1-Hour WordPress 2019

A visual step-by-step guide to building WordPress websites in one hour or less!

Dr. Andy Williams

http://ezseonews.com

Updated 8th November 2018

D1418259

"I work in the education department at one of the top academic institutions in the U.S. and if I could hire Dr. Williams to write all of my online training, I wouldn't hesitate." Laura

Contents

What people are saying about previous versions of this book:

"Complete, quick, and to the point. Just what most people need. Good information. No filler. Great price. A well thought out book by Dr. Andy Williams" **Zoie Brytin**

"This guide or more accurately a manual is an excellent training guide by a teacher that I have been learning from for many years. It is well written and laid out and will help you learn WordPress without stress. Highly recommended." **Dale Reardon**

"By following the steps in the book, you'll easily have your WordPress site up & running in no time and, as Andy knows his stuff, you can be confident it will be set up well." **SBUK**

"Great content from a great author! Highly recommended!" **David H**

"I have read articles which say just set up a WordPress blog and I haven't the faintest idea but this book is very simply and carefully written so no steps are left out. Andy is an expert who seems to be able to explain things in a way which helps the non-expert. A rare talent. It gave me the confidence to have a go." **Chris Wade**

"I think everyone thinking of building a WordPress website should read this guide first. I've been using WordPress for several years and I am amazed at how much I didn't know about WordPress. The guide takes you through the whole process of getting web hosting, buying a domain name, designing your website to help with Search Engine Optimisation and everything else you need to know about posts versus pages, widgets, plugins and lots more. Dr. Andy has a very pleasant writing style which concentrates on what to do and why to do it, without making lots of unnecessary remarks just to fill out a few more pages. And the bonus is that readers get access to his website which he built alongside writing the book and he plans to provide a lot more relevant information there in the future." **John D Bridson**

"The step by step approach is excellent." **Carole**

"Doing anything for the first time can be daunting. Putting up your first WordPress site is no different - especially for the software challenged. Luckily this book offers an easy-to-follow step-by-step process covering all that is needed to overcome any lack of previous experience. With this guide in hand, a new site can realistically be in place in a matter of hours." **John Gergye**

"With this product, it was as if he read my mind (or was watching over my shoulder)." Alan **Northcott**

"The first thing I want to say about "Rapid WordPress Websites" is that you should download it immediately because you need to look no further for information about building your first WordPress website." **Norman Morrison**

"Dr. Andy walks you through the WordPress setup process, step by step. He explains the why's of the steps you are taking, what to do, how to do it, and why you should do it. "Rapid WordPress Websites" is a great instructional refresher guide for even the Pro." **E. W. Aldridge, Sr**

"Anyone who gets this book and follows the steps will be able to have their own website up and running in no time. I hadn't installed a WP blog in years and had forgotten how to do it. Dr. Andy's book made the process simple and painless." **J. Tanner**

"I have been struggling with my WordPress Website - not anymore. This is a must-read for beginners and I bet even some long-time user will find information in Andy's book. I now realize how little I knew about WordPress, the great thing about this book is it walks you by the hand to get your site going and getting down to business. This is one of those books that you will refer to time and time again. So, keep it handy!" **Suzanne Dean**

DISCLAIMER AND TERMS OF USE AGREEMENT

The author and publisher of this eBook and the accompanying materials have used their best efforts in preparing this eBook. The author and publisher make no representation or warranties with respect to the accuracy, applicability, fitness, or completeness of the contents of this eBook. The information contained in this eBook is strictly for educational purposes. Therefore, if you wish to apply ideas contained in this eBook, you are taking full responsibility for your actions.

The author and publisher disclaim any warranties (express or implied), merchantability, or fitness for any particular purpose. The author and publisher shall in no event be held liable to any party for any direct, indirect, punitive, special, incidental or other consequential damages arising directly or indirectly from any use of this material, which is provided "as is", and without warranties.

The author and publisher do not warrant the performance, effectiveness or applicability of any sites listed or linked to in this eBook.

All links are for information purposes only and are not warranted for content, accuracy or any other implied or explicit purpose.

The author and publisher of this book are not in any way associated with Google.

Introduction

Firstly, thank you for buying my book.

This book used to be called "Rapid WordPress Websites". The reason I changed the title of this latest update is simple. I wanted to highlight the fact that you can have your very own WordPress website in an hour or less, from now.

Yes, really.

The aim of this book is to teach anybody (even complete non-techie beginners) to create a website quickly by working through the book, chapter by chapter.

I have written other books on WordPress, but this one is special. The emphasis in this one is to teach you on a need-to-know basis and not try to cover everything that WordPress can do (my WordPress for Beginners book & course both do that).

After reading this book, if you still want more, check out my WordPress books and courses here:

https://ezseonews.com/books

https://ezseonews.com/courses

Special Reader Offer for Video Courses

For readers that like to learn in a more interactive way (and have access to me for Q&A), I've provided discount coupons for my courses on that page above. Just click the link through to the course and the coupon will be applied.

Updates & Changes to WordPress?

The WordPress ecosystem changes a lot. After this book is published, there isn't much I can do to notify you of these changes. I have therefore set up a page on my website for my WordPress-related books, so that updates, changes, and issues, can be listed. If something in the book does not look right, visit the updates page here:

https://ezseonews.com/wp4b/

You can leave comments on that page if you need to.

A Note About UK v US English

There are some differences between UK and US English. While I try to be consistent, some errors may slip into my writing because I spend a lot of time corresponding with people in both the UK and the US. The line can blur.

Examples of this include spelling of words like optimise (UK) v optimize (US).

The difference I get the most complaints about is with collective nouns. Collective nouns refer to a group of individuals, e.g. Google. In the US, collective nouns are singular, so **Google IS** a search engine. However, in the UK, collective nouns are usually plural, so **Google ARE** a search engine.

There are other differences too. I hope that if I have been inconsistent anywhere in this book, it does not detract from the value you get from it.

WordPress itself will have some differences depending on whether you are using UK or US English. The one I find most obvious is in the labeling of the areas containing things you have deleted. E.g. comments, or posts/pages.

If you installed WordPress with US English, you'll see this called "trash":

But if your WordPress is installed with UK English this becomes "bin":

In this book, I largely use Bin (as I am in the UK and speak proper English 😊), but you will still see the occasional screenshot that uses the word Trash.

Found Typos in This Book?

Errors can get through proof-readers, so if you do find any typos or grammatical errors in this book, I'd be very grateful if you could let me know using this email address:

typos@ezseonews.com

WordPress.com v WordPress.org

The first thing that confuses many WordPress students is that there are two types of WordPress. These are found on two separate websites.

If you visit WordPress.com, you can sign up to create a WordPress site for free. WordPress.com hosts your site on their servers, meaning you do not need to buy a domain, or hosting. The downside is that there are limitations. WordPress.com controls what you can and cannot do on your site. For example, you won't be able to customize WordPress in the way you want, because you cannot just install any theme or plugin you want. You also won't be using your own domain name. Your website address will be something like:

myhealthsite.WordPress.com

This type of domain is called a sub-domain and it is hosted on the WordPress.com website. Therefore, you do not own the domain and WordPress.com could theoretically close your site down if they think you are abusing their terms of service.

There are paid options on WordPress.com which allow you to use your own domain, but the price for doing so is greater than if you just use WordPress.org in the first place and unless you are on the most expensive plan, there will still be restrictions.

I don't recommend WordPress.com for building sites, but if you decide you want to try, I have a course on using this free service. You can find discounted links to all my courses at the end of this book.

WordPress.org, on the other hand, is a site where you can download the WordPress software for yourself, to install on a server of your choice, and customize it however you wish. This allows you to create a website that you own, and you can do whatever you want on it. You also get to choose your own domain name, like:

myhealthsite.com

Doesn't that look better? Be aware that domain names are on a strictly first come, first served basis. You obviously cannot choose a domain name that someone else already owns.

In this book, we are using the WordPress from WordPress.org, buying a domain name, and building the site on our own web host.

NOTE: It is possible to install WordPress on your own computer if you just want to learn without the expense of buying a domain and subscribing to a web host. Obviously, that is beyond the scope of this book, so check out those courses (the one called "Installing WordPress Locally") at the end of this book if you are interested.

Let's get started...

Domains, Registrars & Hosting

Your domain name is important to you. It will be your website address where you can send your friends & family to view your site. It is the website address that Google and other search engines will send people to. Therefore, choosing a domain name is important, and you want to get it right the first time. You cannot get a refund on a purchased domain name if you find you made a spelling mistake or changed your mind about the name.

Two types of domain name

There are two main types of domain name. The first category, which I suggest you avoid, is often referred to as "Exact Match Domain", or EMD for short.

An EMD is a domain name that exactly matches a phrase you want to rank for in Google. For example, if you decide you wanted to be #1 on Google when anyone searched for "Healthy Coconut Oil", then an EMD would be something like:

- Healthycoconutoil.com
- Healthy-coconut-oil.com
- Healthcocounutoil.org

See how the exact phrase makes up the domain name?

This used to work well in Google, and in the past, we could easily rank sites for phrases by choosing an EMD for the phrase we were interested in. However, things have changed. EMDs can cause you problems, including getting your site penalized in Google, or even banned if you are not careful.

I, therefore, suggest you choose my second category of domain name – a brandable name.

A brandable domain name is one that is memorable and could be used as branding. Think of Google itself. This is a brand name we all recognize, but what would have happened if they had chosen "best search engine" as an EMD? Bestsearchengine.com doesn't have the same ring to it, does it?

I recommend you sit down and think about your domain name carefully. Avoid choosing a name simply because it contains a phrase you want to rank for. Instead, think of a memorable name that people will remember when they hear it.

Imagine being out and about and you see a friend. You want to send them over to look at your new website but you don't have a pencil to write the name down. The domain name you choose should be memorable enough that your friend can remember it once you tell them.

TLDs

TLD stands for Top Level Domain and simply refers to the extension given to your domain. Possible TLDs include .com, .org, .net, .co.uk, .de etc. There are new TLDs coming out on a regular basis and it can all be confusing for beginners.

Some TLDs are country-specific, e.g. ".co.uk" is used for websites targeting the UK.

My advice on choosing a TLD is simple.

If you only want to target one country with your site, choose the TLD for that country:

.es for Spain

.co.uk for the UK

.de for Germany

If your site has a global appeal, choose a .com.

How much is it all going to cost?

Since we need to buy a domain and hosting, you may already be wondering how much this is going to cost. Let me break it down for you:

You need to buy a domain name which will cost around $9.99 per year. You buy domain names from "domain registrars" (see below).

You need to get web hosting, and that costs from around $3.99 per month. You buy web hosting from a "web host" (see below).

These are your only required costs, though obviously, you can decide to buy a premium WordPress theme and maybe some commercial plugins. However, these are not required, and you can build a great looking, feature-packed site, without any additional costs.

Your total essential costs for a self-hosted website will be around $58 per year. That's not bad considering you'll be able to get your message out to the entire connected world.

What is a Domain Registrar?

A domain registrar is a company that you buy your domain name from. Good registrars will make sure your domain auto-renews at the end of the year, can keep your site "anonymous", lock your domain so it cannot be transferred to another individual without your approval, and a lot of other administrative stuff.

What is a Web host?

A web host is a company that rents out computer space to anyone that wants to create their own website. They are responsible for making sure your site is up and running 24/7. All websites can go down at times (as I am sure you have seen), but good web hosts will have your website up and running 99.9% of the time.

All-in-one registrar and web host?

Most web hosts will also offer to be your domain registrar. In other words, they look after everything for you. The advantage of this is that everything is in one place, and you are only dealing with one company.

The disadvantage of this is that if you have problems with your host, they hold all the cards, and can make moving away from them difficult. I have heard horror stories about some hosts.

The thing about web hosts is that they might be great today, but suck tomorrow. I have seen several great hosts go downhill quickly. Being able to move your site quickly if you ever need to is important.

I want you to avoid potential problems down the line by doing things right from the start, so I am going to show you how to use a separate host and registrar.

Before you start thinking that a separate registrar and host is more complicated, it really isn't. It's also no more expensive. In fact, the registrar I will recommend to you is free to use.

I will show you how to painlessly and easily set up your domain so that that you are using a separate domain registrar and hosting company. You are then in control. If you ever need to move from one web host to another, the process is very simple, and your site can be moved within hours, with zero downtime.

My Recommended Web Host and Registrar

As you might guess from the information above, I do change my web hosts occasionally. What I recommend today may not be what I recommend in a year's time. Therefore, to make sure you are using the absolute best services that I know of (the ones I personally use), I recommend you visit my page here to check:

http://ezseonews.com/host

I will keep it updated if there are any changes.

At the time of writing this book, my chosen registrar is Namecheap and my chosen Web host is StableHost. I have been happily using both for several years now, without issue. I will show you how to set up a site using these two services (and even get you a 40% discount on your web hosting).

Visit http://ezseonews.com/host

Click on the link for my recommended Registrar. Sign up for a free account. Once you have that account set up, come back here and we will continue.

Buying the domain at the registrar

Over at the registrar (Namecheap), we want to buy a new domain.

From the Domains menu at the top, select **Domain Name Search**:

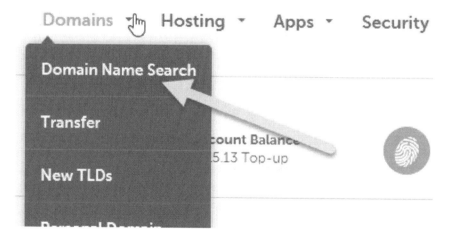

You can then type in your chosen domain name (with TLD) and click the search button to see if it is available.

My chosen domain is available:

If the domain is available, you'll see a check mark next to it at the top of the page. Click the shopping trolley button to add the domain to your cart.

View the cart and make sure your domain is correct (check the spelling).

At the checkout, make sure you enable **Auto-Renew** for the domain.

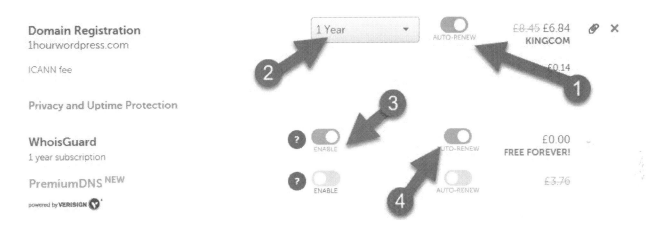

This will ensure that the registrar will automatically renew your domain name each year (until you cancel). Failure to renew a domain will result in your domain being released when the year is up, and someone else will be able to buy it.

When you buy your domain, you can buy it for longer than one year if you want to. If you have auto-renew enabled, I see no reason to buy for longer than one year.

You will also be offered WhoisGuard which is now permanently free on Namecheap. WhoisGuard protects your name, address, phone number and other contact details from the Whois.net database. Anyone can search this database online (at http://whois.net) to find contact details for the owner of a website. If you want the privacy provided by this, it's a good option to include.

When you are happy with your selection, click the confirm order button to buy your domain.

If you got the WhoisGuard as well, there will be a link asking you to activate it on the domain. Just follow the instructions there.

OK; that's the registrar done.

Let's head over to the web hosting company.

Visit this page again, and click through to the recommended web host:

http://ezseonews.com/host

If my recommendation is still StableHost, check for a discount code I've included on that page which will give you a 40% discount on hosting (I cannot guarantee how long this will be available).

Buying Web hosting

The exact process will depend on the hosting you buy, but I will cover the process on Stablehost in this book. If my recommendation is no longer Stablehost, then look on the recommended page above, and I'll cover a guide on how to sign up for my recommended host.

OK, back to Stablehost. On the web hosting page, which you can access from the menu across the top, you can sign up for hosting:

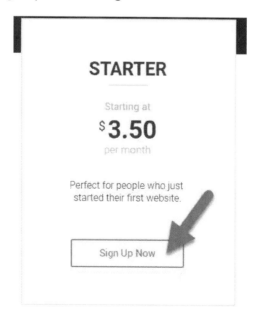

I recommend you use the Starter plan, to begin with. If your site becomes very popular, or you decide to build other sites, you can always upgrade to a more comprehensive plan when you need to.

When you click the **Sign Up Now** button, you will be taken to the product selection screen:

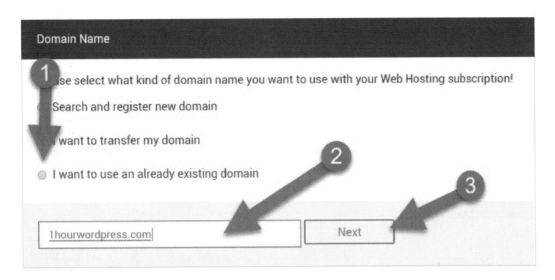

Select the option to use your existing domain as this one lets you use a different registrar. Enter the domain name and the extension in the box provided. Click the **Next** button to view your cart.

Web hosts often give incentives for paying for hosting up front. With Stablehost, as I write this, if you want to sign up for 6 months or less, it will cost you $4.95 per month. However, if you pay for 36 months up front, it'll only cost you $3.50 per month.

I recommend paying for as long a period as you feel comfortable with, as any discount you get from the coupon on my site will apply to the amount you are paying now. I'll select 36 months to show you.

Product	Type	Period	Price	
Unlimited Starter	Hosting	36 Months - $3.50 ▾	$ 3.50	✖ Remove
Phoenix, USA - StableHost Cluster ▾	Hosting Location		$ 0.00	
SSH Access	Addon		$ 2.50	✖ Remove
1hourwordpress.com	Own Domain	1 Year Own	$ 0.00	✖ Remove

You need to choose here is the hosting location. You can choose from Phoenix, Amsterdam, Chicago and Stockholm. Your website will be served from the server in the location you choose, so select the place closest to where you think your target audience is located. If you are unsure, just select Phoenix.

You don't need to buy the SSH Access in your package, so click the remove button to delete that.

Further down the screen, you'll see the total to pay now:

Price:	$ 126.00
Total pay:	$ 126.00
Coupon Code:	Apply!

As you can see, the full cost for 36 months hosting is 126.00. However, remember that coupon code. Enter that in the coupon code box on the page and click the **Apply** button. After a few seconds, your shopping cart will be updated showing a 40% discount on the total:

Price:	$ 126.00
Discount:	$ 50.40
Total pay:	$ 75.60
Coupon Code:	Apply!

The above screenshot shows that the promotional code would save over $50 on this hosting package.

Instead of costing $126.00, it's just $75.60!

Go through to the checkout and pay for your hosting.

It may take a few hours for your hosting to be set up. Once it is, the host will email you with login details for your cPanel (which you'll need for setting up WordPress). You will also have login details for your "Client Login", and it's in there you can get support if you need it.

The other thing you'll get in your welcome email is the Server information. This is what you are looking for:

Server Information

Server Name: en01.stablehost.com

If you are using an existing domain with your new hosting ac
below.

Nameserver 1 ns1.stablehost.com (199.192.218.10)
Nameserver 2 ns2.stablehost.com (199.192.219.10)

Uploading Your Website

There are two Nameservers. If you are using Stablehost, they'll be the same as in the screenshot above.

We will need these in the next step.

Connecting the Registrar and host

Login to your registrar (Namecheap).

From the menu on the top left, select **Domain List.**

You will see your domain listed. Click on the **Manage** button to the right of the domain name.

You will be on the **Domain Details** tab, so scroll down until you see the Nameservers section:

Change the top drop-down box to **Custom DNS** and then enter the two nameservers (that we located in the previous section) in boxes 1 & 2.

Finally, click the **Save** button that looks like a little check mark (tick).

That's it. The registrar and the web host will now work together. Not that difficult, was it?

Now we can go and install WordPress on the domain.

Installing WordPress

For this, you need to login to the cPanel of your web host. The URL, username, and password were all in that welcome email the host sent to you.

Once you are logged in, scroll down to the **Softaculous Apps Installer** section, and click on **WordPress**.

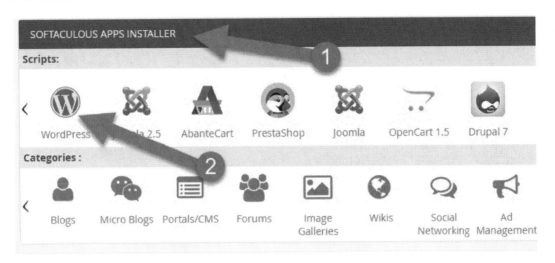

You'll be taken to the WordPress Installation screen:

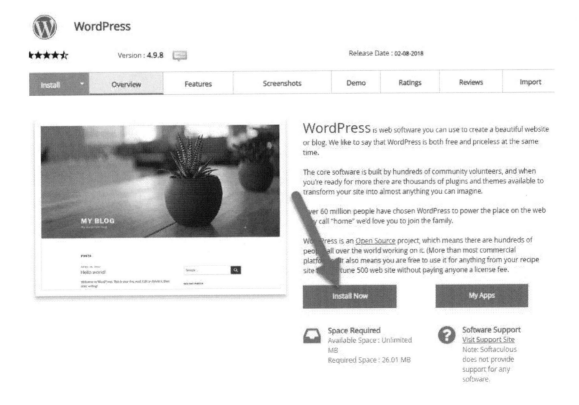

Click the **Install Now** button.

At the top of the next screen, you'll see the **Software Setup**:

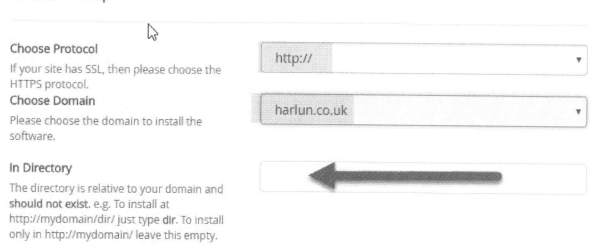

In the **Choose Protocol** box, select http://

In the **Choose Domain** box, select your domain.

Clear the **In Directory** box by deleting the pre-filled value.

The next section of this screen is the **Site Settings**.

Site Settings

Site Name	Harlun Limited
Site Description	My Company Website
Enable Multisite (WPMU) ⓘ	☐

Enter a name and short description (tagline) for your site. Don't worry, you can change these later.

Make sure **Enable Multisite** is unchecked.

In the **Admin Account** section, enter a username, password, and the email address you want to use for this website.

Admin Account

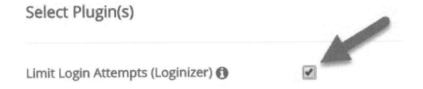

Admin Username   admin

Admin Password   pass   Hide

Bad (18/100)

Admin Email   admin@harlun.co.uk

Do not use "admin" as the username. Use something a little harder to guess, and the same goes for the password.

The next section allows you to choose your language and then there is a **Select Plugin** section.

The plugin that is available is called Limit Login Attempts, and it can help prevent hackers gaining access to your site, so check that box.

Select Plugin(s)

Limit Login Attempts (Loginizer) ⓘ   ☑

The final section on this page is the **Advanced Options**. Open them by clicking the "+".

➕ Advanced Options

I recommend you enable the following:

- Auto Upgrade
- Auto Upgrade WordPress Plugins
- Auto Upgrade WordPress Themes

Finally, before clicking the **Install** button, enter an email address to receive the installation details. Once WordPress is installed, the username and password will be sent to this address.

With all that complete, click the **Install** button.

Once the installation has finished, you'll be shown something like this:

Congratulations, the software was installed successfully

WordPress has been successfully installed at :
http://harlun.co.uk
Administrative URL : http://harlun.co.uk/wp-admin/

We hope the installation process was easy.

The first link will load your website which is now actually online. Congratulations! It may not be much yet, but you have created your very first WordPress website!

Here is mine:

The default WordPress site you see will use the current WordPress default "theme". Think of a theme as a skin to your site, that can be changed. Every theme is different, and by changing the theme, you can change the entire look and feel of your website.

At the time of writing this, the default theme was Twenty Seventeen, so that is the theme you see in the screenshot above. Yours may show a different theme, but that is fine. You'll want to play with themes later and choose one that you like.

The second URL listed is the Administrative URL.

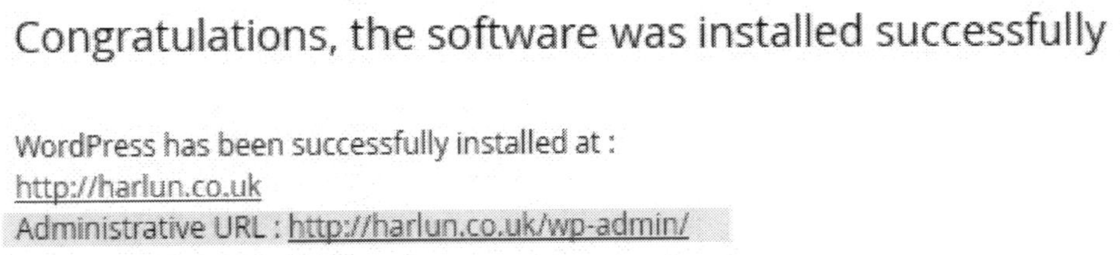

Congratulations, the software was installed successfully

WordPress has been successfully installed at :
http://harlun.co.uk
Administrative URL : http://harlun.co.uk/wp-admin/

You can click that link to login to the WordPress Dashboard for your site.

Bookmark the URL for your Dashboard. You will need it whenever you want to go in and work on your website.

The username and password are those that you used when filling in the Admin Details a few minutes ago.

OK, let's log in to the Dashboard.

Login and Logout of your WordPress Dashboard

The WordPress Dashboard is where you go to add content and customize the look of your site. Think of it as the control center for your website.

You should have bookmarked the URL already, but if you ever forget or lose your admin link, just add **/wp-admin/** to the end of your domain URL.

This is what the login page looks like:

Enter your Admin username and Admin password. I recommend you check the **Remember Me** box so that it remembers your login details next time.

Now click the **Log In** button.

You will be taken inside the dashboard. Here is mine:

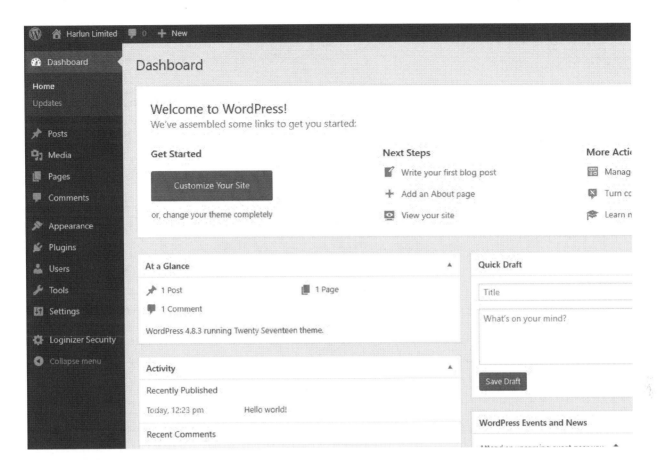

OK, this is where the fun starts.

Looking at the demo page, post, and comment

.. and deleting them

When you install WordPress, you will get some demo content installed by default. This includes:

- A post
- A page
- A comment

Don't worry about posts and pages, we will discuss them later. For now, let's take a quick look.

Visit your site in a web browser. You can do this in a number of different ways.

Obviously, you can type the domain URL into the web browser.

If you are already in your dashboard, move your mouse over your domain name (top left). Now right-click the **Visit** Site link and select **Open link in a new tab.**

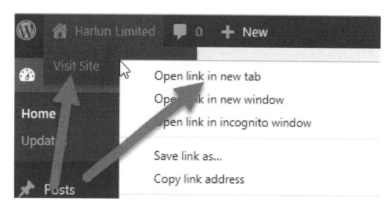

Your website will open in a new tab.

This is your homepage and you should see a post titled "Hello World".

POSTS

NOVEMBER 6, 2018 EDIT

Hello world!

Welcome to WordPress. This is your first post. Edit or delete it, then start writing!

A note on the homepage

The homepage is a special page. By default, WordPress will show your most recent 10 posts on the homepage (there is only one on your homepage right now because there is only one post on your site - the "Hello World" post).

The homepage can display the full post(s), or what is called excerpts. What it shows depends on the WordPress theme you are using and how you set it up. While the latest posts appear on the Homepage, you should also know that they also each appear on their own "post page". If you click the "Hello World!" title shown in the screenshot above, you will be taken to the post's page.

This page contains the single post in its entirety, any comments on the post, and a "Leave a Reply" comment box for visitors to leave a comment.

Here is the "Hello World!" post page on my site:

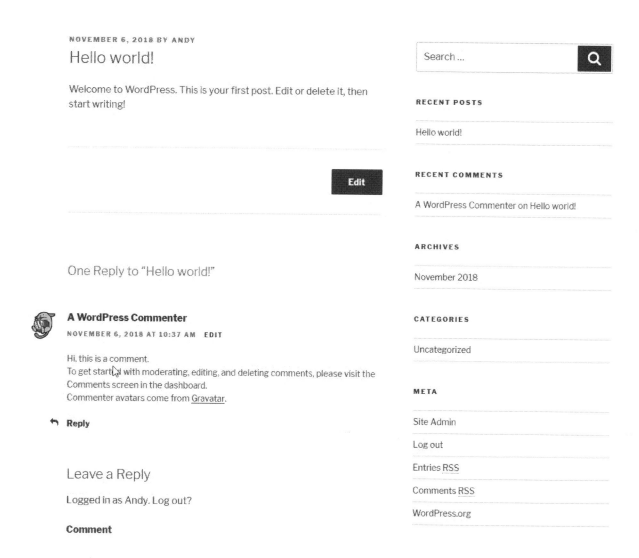

NOVEMBER 6, 2018 BY ANDY

Hello world!

Welcome to WordPress. This is your first post. Edit or delete it, then start writing!

Edit

One Reply to "Hello world!"

A WordPress Commenter
NOVEMBER 6, 2018 AT 10:37 AM   EDIT

Hi, this is a comment.
To get started with moderating, editing, and deleting comments, please visit the Comments screen in the dashboard.
Commenter avatars come from Gravatar.

↩ Reply

Leave a Reply

Logged in as Andy. Log out?

Comment

Search … 🔍

RECENT POSTS

Hello world!

RECENT COMMENTS

A WordPress Commenter on Hello world!

ARCHIVES

November 2018

CATEGORIES

Uncategorized

META

Site Admin

Log out

Entries RSS

Comments RSS

WordPress.org

NOTE: If you don't like the idea of the homepage showing the last 10 posts, and you'd rather have a carefully crafted homepage "article", you can do that. I'll show you how to set up a static homepage soon.

If you go back to the homepage, you'll see a sidebar. In the Twenty Seventeen theme, the sidebar is on the right (see screenshot above).

Some themes will have the sidebar on the left, and others won't have a sidebar.

You can see that "Hello World!" is listed in the sidebar in a section called **Recent Posts**.

There is also a section called **Recent Comments**, with one entry:

RECENT COMMENTS

A WordPress Commenter on Hello world!

When WordPress was installed, it added this "Hello World!" post and the comment (on that post) as a kind of demo for you. If you go to the Hello World post page, you can see the comment at the end:

One Reply to "Hello world!"

 A WordPress Commenter

NOVEMBER 6, 2018 AT 10:37 AM   EDIT

Hi, this is a comment.
To get started with moderating, editing, and deleting comments, please visit the Comments screen in the dashboard.
Commenter avatars come from Gravatar.

↰ **Reply**

Leave a Reply

Logged in as Andy. Log out?

Comment

You'll also see other sections in the sidebar, including Archives, Categories, and Meta. These sidebar sections are inserted into the sidebar using something called "Widgets". We'll look at these later, but just so you know, you can add or delete widgets in the sidebar, so it is highly customizable.

When you installed WordPress, a "Page" was also installed. We can find that in the dashboard, as well as the post and comment.

Login to the Dashboard.

A quick way to get into the Dashboard is to use the admin bar across the top. This will appear when you are viewing your site but logged into the dashboard already. Here it is:

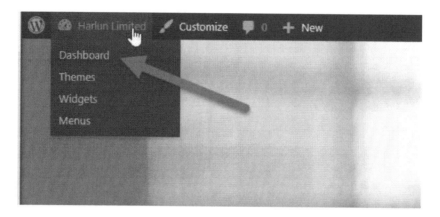

Move your mouse over the domain name and click on **Dashboard** to get in.

On logging in, you'll have a menu down the left:

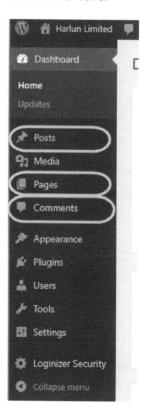

You can see the menu items for "Posts", "Pages" and "Comments".

Click on the Posts menu item and you'll be taken to a screen listing all posts on the site.

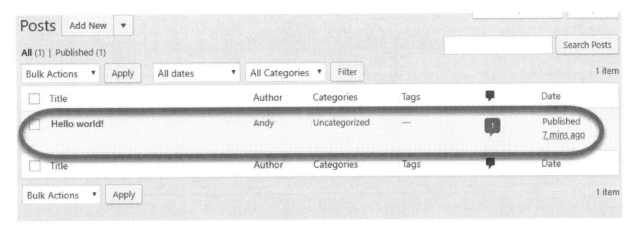

Now, there's only one - the "Hello World" post. No surprise there as we haven't added any yet. If you want to go in and edit the Hello World post, click on the title and you'll be taken to the post edit screen.

OK, click on the "Comments" menu in the left sidebar.

This screen looks like the last one. All the comments on the site are listed. At the moment, there is just the one that WordPress installed.

The "In Response To" column tells you where the comment was left. You can see that this comment was left in the Hello World post. You can click on the "Hello World" title to be taken to that post, open in the edit post screen. What you see here will depend on whether you are using the classic WYSIWYG editor that was standard in WordPress version 4 and earlier:

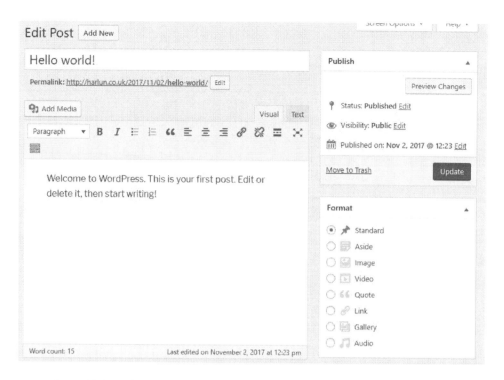

However, version 5.0 of WordPress introduced the Gutenberg editor, which is completely different. If you are still using v4.x of WordPress, you can install the Gutenberg editor as a plugin if you want. Anyway, the Hello World post in the Gutenberg editor looks like this:

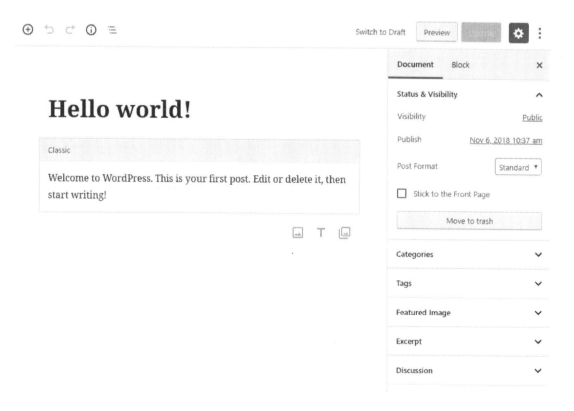

We will look at these two editors later in the book.

Deleting the Demo Post & Comment

To delete a post, click on **All Posts** inside the **Posts** menu in the dashboard sidebar.

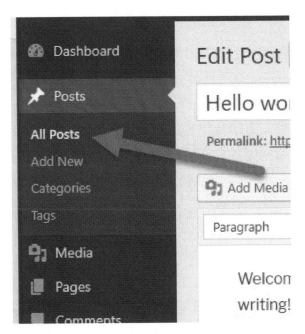

You'll see a list of all posts on the site. Find the one you want to delete, and move your mouse over the title:

You'll see a menu that offers a **Trash** link. Click it. Once deleted, you'll see that your list of posts now shows (1) in Trash:

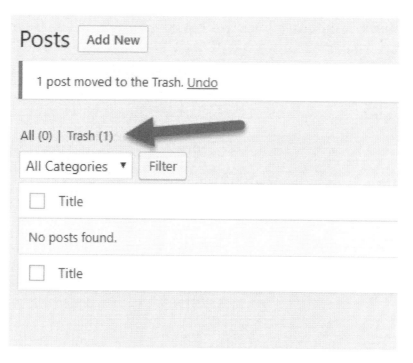

If you click the **Trash (1)** link, you'll open the trash:

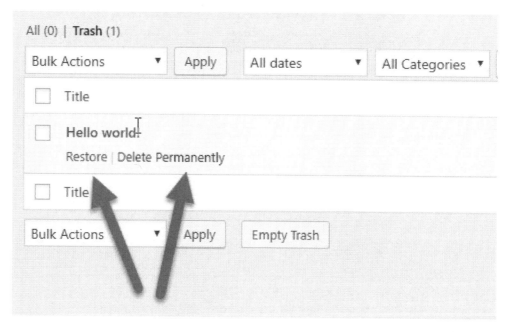

The trash contains all posts you've deleted (assuming you haven't emptied the trash), so you can see the Hello World post. The trash acts as a safety net. If you decide you want to restore a post you've deleted, you can. Or you can delete permanently.

There is another way to delete posts. To demonstrate this, I'll restore the Hello World post from the trash by clicking the **Restore** link.

Once restored, go back to the "All Posts" list again. There is the post, back from trash.

Check the box next to the post(s) you want to delete and select **Move to Trash** from the drop-down box.

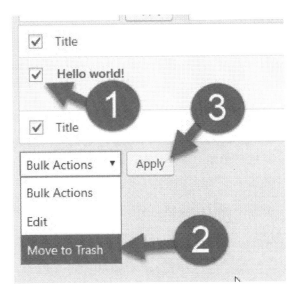

Then click the **Apply** button to move the selected posts to the trash.

This method of deleting posts is useful if you want to delete several posts. A similar system works in the comments section. You can delete comments one by one, or select several comments and send them all to the Trash in one go.

OK, now let's look at the Pages that WordPress installed. Click the Pages menu item in the left sidebar.

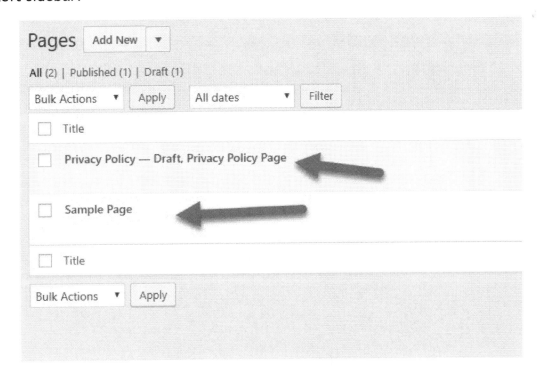

It's a familiar looking screen, isn't it? It's very similar to the screen for posts and for comments.

WordPress created two sample pages. One is a draft you can use for a privacy policy; the other is a sample page.

Click the **Sample Page** title to open the page in the Page editor.

You'll see that the main editor window is the same as the one for posts, though other options on this screen are different. We'll look at those later. Click the back button on your browser to go back to the "all pages" list.

Delete the Page in the same way you deleted the "Hello World!" post. The page will go to the page trash, which you can go into if you need to restore a page.

OK, we've deleted the post, which also deleted the comment associated with the post. We've also deleted the page. Therefore, the site is now empty:

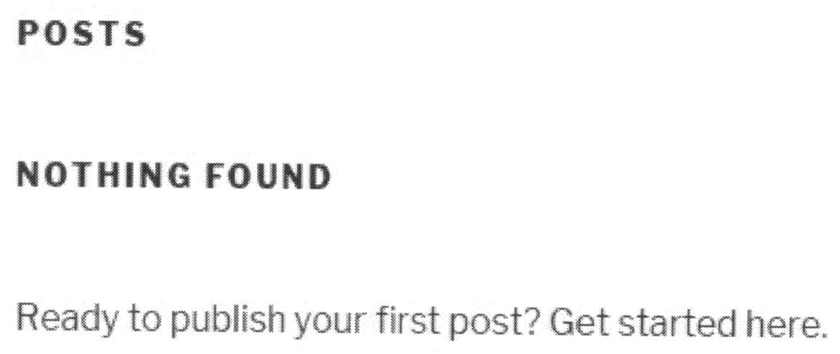

POSTS

NOTHING FOUND

Ready to publish your first post? Get started here.

You have an empty site, now you need to add your content.

Planning the site

We've got a skeleton site, with no content. The first thing I suggest you do is to plan out what you want to include on your site. What content do you want to publish there?

You don't have to decide on everything just yet, but having a good plan before you start will make things a lot easier.

WordPress is so flexible that you can use it to create just about any type of website.

For example, let's consider this basic model for a site about WordPress:

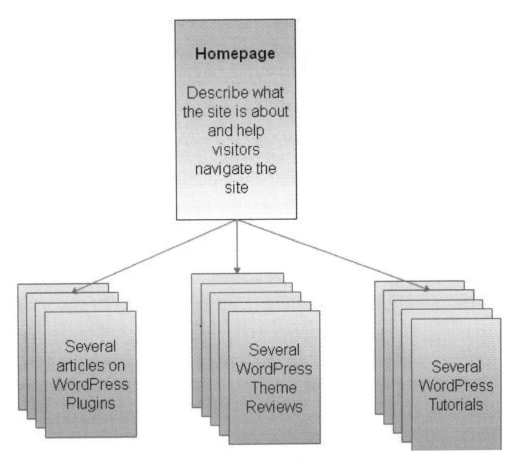

The homepage will introduce the site to my visitors and tell them what the site is about. The homepage will also help my visitors find what they are looking for. The site will have three main sections (for now, at least, but this may increase over time). There will be a section with several articles on WordPress plugins, another section with articles on WordPress themes, and then some WordPress tutorials.

In addition to this website "content", here are a few other things you need:

1. About Us page (for the visitors, and Google likes to see one).
2. Contact Us form (for the visitors and Google likes to see one)
3. Privacy Policy (for a little legal coverage)
4. Terms of Use (for a little legal coverage).

From the above, we can see that there are two distinct types of content.

There are those articles that we are writing to engage our visitors on the topic of our site, in this case, WordPress. These articles can typically and conveniently be grouped into "categories" and we will call this type of article **"website content"**.

The other type of content is the stuff that is not directly related to the topic of the site but is required to make the site complete and more professional (as well as provide ourselves with a little legal protection). This type of content is what I call the "legal pages". These "legal" pages are typically very similar for all sites you build, irrespective of topic.

This is where the difference between WordPress posts and WordPress pages should start to become obvious.

"Website content" is created as WordPress "posts".

"Legal pages" are created as WordPress "pages".

We'll look at this in more detail, but before we do, there are a few WordPress settings we need to change.

Getting the House in Order

WordPress comes installed with a number of default settings that really aren't in our best interests. In this section, we will make some changes and set up a few things. We are getting our house in order, ready for the first content.

WordPress Settings

I won't cover all the settings in WordPress, just the ones that are important at this stage. Follow along and make the changes as we go through them.

Checkpoint #1 – Author Profile

From the Users menu in the left sidebar, select **Your Profile**.

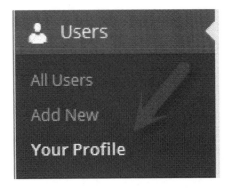

At the top of the screen, you'll see some personal options:

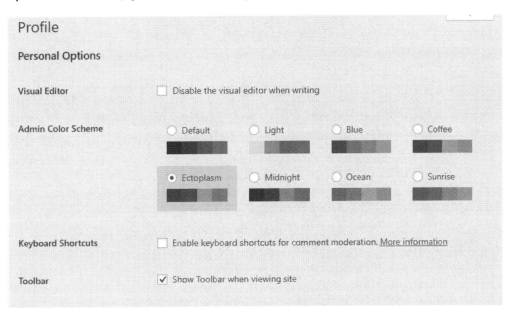

Make sure the "Disable the visual editor when writing" option is unchecked. Checking this option would remove the WYSIWYG editor from WordPress making it more difficult to create nicely formatted content.

The admin color scheme is a personal taste thing, so play around with the colors if you wish.

The "Show Toolbar when viewing site" should also be checked. This will place an admin bar across the top of your browser window when you are viewing your site while logged into your Dashboard. This admin bar gives you quick access to several dashboard features.

Underneath, you need to enter a few personal details.

Name

Username	andy	Usernames cannot be changed.
First Name	Andy	
Last Name	Williams	
Nickname (required)	Andy	
Display name publicly as	Andy ▼	

Contact Info

Email (required)	webmaster@ezseonews.com
Website	http://ezseonews.com

You cannot edit the username, so that box is greyed out.

Enter your first and last name.

In the Nickname, enter whatever you like. It will be prefilled with your username, but you can change it.

In the **Display name publicly as**, select the way you want your name appearing on the website. The options available will include combinations of your first and last name, nickname, username etc.

Make sure you have a valid email address in the contact info box.

Finally, on this screen, add a little information about yourself in the **Biographical Info** box.

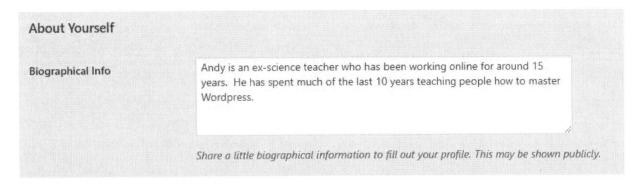

This information may be used on your website, e.g. as an author bio after posts (depending on the theme). Here is the author bio after the Hello World post using the Twenty Sixteen theme (themes are like "skins" for your site and we'll look at them later):

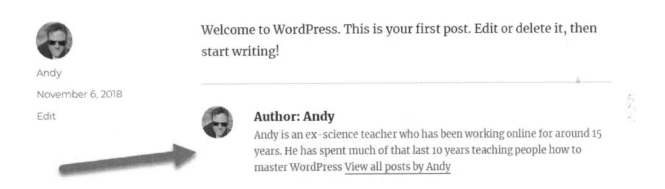

It may also be used as an introduction to your author page (a page that WordPress creates to highlight all content you, as an author, have written on the site).

Incidentally, if you want to find your own author page, visit a "post page" and look for your author name under the title:

Hello world!

Andy

November 6, 2018

Edit

Welcome to WordPress. This is your first post. E‹ start writing!

Not all themes will show this, but if it does show your "display name", click it to be taken to your author page.

Checkpoint #2 - Update Services

Go to **Writing** in the **Settings** menu in the left sidebar.

You will see a large box labeled **Update Services** (also referred to as a ping list). At the moment, there is just one entry.

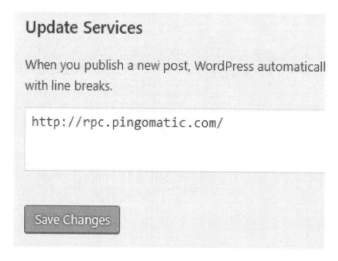

Essentially, whenever you post new content (or update an existing article) on your site, each of the sites listed in the update service list will be notified. This can mean your content gets indexed and included in the search engines within minutes. However, we can do better than just one update service.

Do a Google search for **WordPress update services + current year**, and find a list someone else has put together.

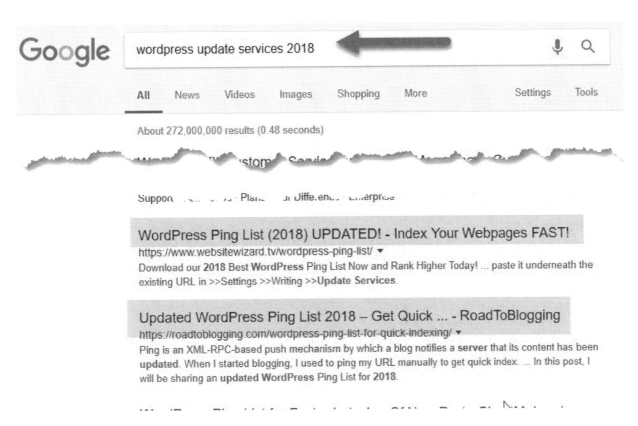

Copy and paste the list (as plain text) into your own "ping list", and save.

Each URL in the list needs to be on a separate line.

Checkpoint #3 - Reading Settings

Go to **Reading** in the **Settings** menu in the left sidebar:

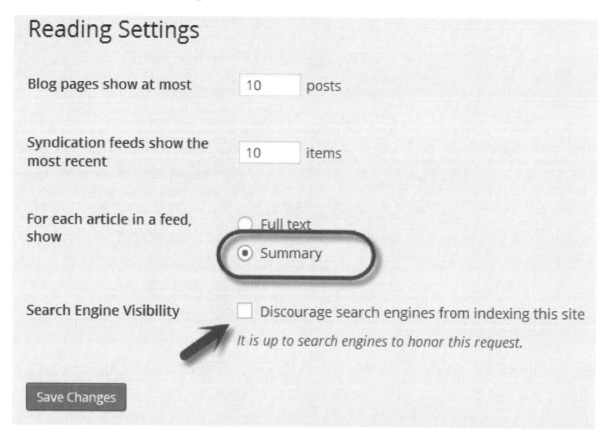

Make sure that **Summary** is selected, and that the search engine visibility box is UNCHECKED. If you check this option, the search engines WILL NOT index your pages or include them in the search engines. This can be useful if you don't want your site showing up in the search engines until you are ready, but I advise you to leave it unchecked. Google will come and see the site being actively developed, and this will encourage Google to come back frequently to spider and index your content.

Checkpoint #4 - Discussion Settings

Go to **Discussion** in the **Settings** menu in the left sidebar.

Most of these options can be left as they are. The ones to change are listed below:

Change 1:

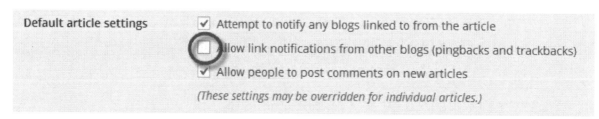

Uncheck the option above, to help prevent spammy "comments" on your site.

Change 2:

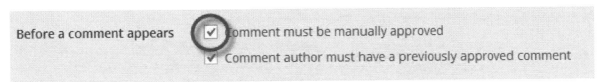

Check the option to manually approve all comments.

Change 3:

The comment blacklist will help sort out a lot of spam comments before you even see them. You simply enter all the words you want to be considered spam, and if those words appear in a comment, the comment is marked as spam and sent to the spam folder.

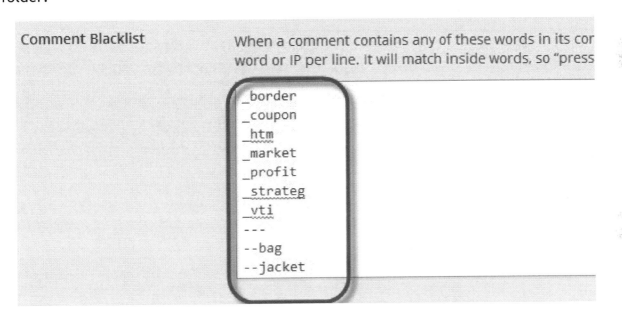

You don't have to think of the words yourself as others have created lists for us. Do a Google search for **WordPress comment blacklist**. Find a list you can copy and paste into your own comment blacklist.

Change 4:

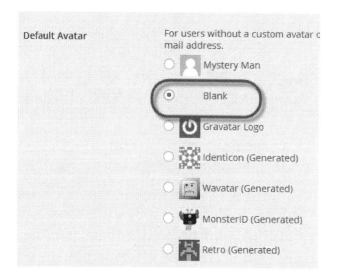

Under the default Avatar section, select **Blank**.

Reason: If someone leaving a comment does not have a Gravatar set up (this is an image associated with their email address), then we don't want an image displayed with their comment.

You can set it up to use any of those other images as the default image, but by using an image, you are slowing down the load times of your web pages.

Checkpoint #5 – Permalinks

Under the **Settings** menu, go to **Permalinks**.

This is an important one.

The permalink structure will determine how the URLs of your site look when a page loads in a web browser.

For example, if you have the "plain" option selected, the URL for the Hello World post will look something like this:

P is the number of the post in the WordPress database. As this is the first post, the **post ID** of "hello world" is 1. That URL doesn't offer much to a visitor or search engine.

From a search engine point of view, it is far better to be more descriptive with your URLs. What I recommend you do is add the category and post name to the URL. Don't worry what that means right now, just make the following change:

Select **Custom Structure**, and delete whatever is currently in the edit box:

Once empty, click on the %category% and then %postname% buttons so that your permalink structure now looks like this:

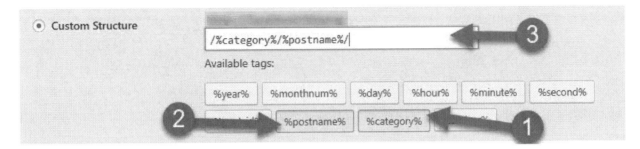

Save your changes.

To give you an idea of what this has done, look at the URL of the hello world post now:

The word "Uncategorized" in the URL is the category of the "Hello World" post, which is currently called "Uncategorized" (the default category installed by WordPress). Of course, when we come to add content to our site, we will give our categories meaningful names.

Checkpoint #6 – Plugins

Click on the Plugins menu in the left sidebar. There will be a few plugins that were installed with WordPress.

The first is Akismet Anti-Spam.

Akismet is a plugin that helps prevent comment spam, and it is extremely effective at what it does. However, if your site is commercial in nature (you make any money from the site), then you need the paid version of this plugin. Akismet can only be used for free if your site is a personal, non-profit website. If that's you, then click the "Activate" link under the plugin to "turn it on", and then head on over to Akismet to setup your account. See the Akismet site for details on how to do this.

If you are not going to be using a plugin, you should delete it, since leaving unused plugins on your server can increase the security risk of your site. Old plugins can have vulnerabilities that hackers use, and if you have old and unused plugins with these vulnerabilities on your server, you are a target.

To delete a plugin, click the delete link under the plugin.

Hello Dolly can be deleted, as can Akismet if you are not using it.

Checkpoint #7 - Gravatars

We mentioned Gravatars earlier. They are images that we can associate with our email address. If you look at the top right of your Dashboard, you will see your name and a placeholder image where your photo could be. Here is mine:

My photo is appearing there because I am using a Gravatar associated with my admin email address. If I use that email to post a comment on any other blog, my photo appears with my comment. Here is an example:

- high relevance to site theme

I had not thought about the nofollow link but now you've got me thinking.

I would appreciate your views on this
Many thanks & regards

Reply

Andy Williams says
17/3/2014 AT 08:25 (EDIT)

It's good to have a plan like this, and overall I like it, but I wou allow the following links on a Guest post.
1. Dofollow to Google Plus profile page. This would be dofol that authorship could be established. I don't know if anything changed, but when I tried several months ago, authorship wo work if the profile link was nofollow

In the screenshot, I am replying to a comment. My Gravatar shows because I used my admin email when I commented.

Gravatars are a great way to brand yourself and I highly recommend you use a Gravatar for your own Admin email address. Visitors to your site love to know who they are dealing with, so get over your shyness and put your face on your site.

To sign up for a Gravatar, head on over to https://en.gravatar.com/

Look for the link to **Create your own Gravatar**, and follow the instructions. Now, whenever you post a comment on any website that is related to your own, use the email address that has your Gravatar attached, and your face will show up next to your comments on these other sites (unless they have Gravatars disabled, but very few do).

Checkpoint #8 - Adding a Sitemap

A sitemap is essentially a list of pages on your site, and it is used mainly by the search engines to find all your content. It is, therefore, a good idea to have one. The best way to add a sitemap is to use a plugin.

Click on **Add New** in the **Plugins** sidebar menu.

Search for **Yoast SEO** and find this plugin by Team Yoast:

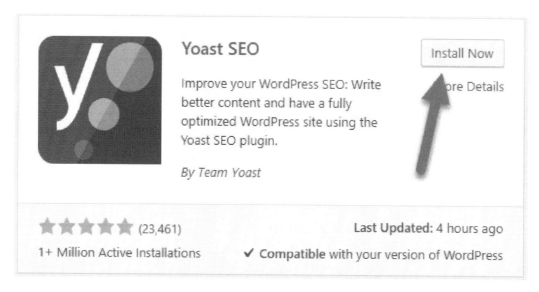

Click the **Install Now.**

Once installed, click the **Activate** button that replaced the "install now" button.

You will now have a new sidebar menu:

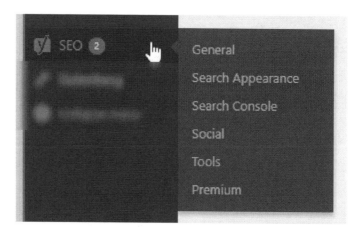

As the menu title suggests, this plugin is more than a sitemap plugin. It's a very flexible and useful SEO plugin. It is beyond the scope of this book to teach you how to set this up, but I will show you how to activate the sitemap.

Click on the **General** menu item.

The General screen loads, with three tabs across the top. Click on the **Features** tab:

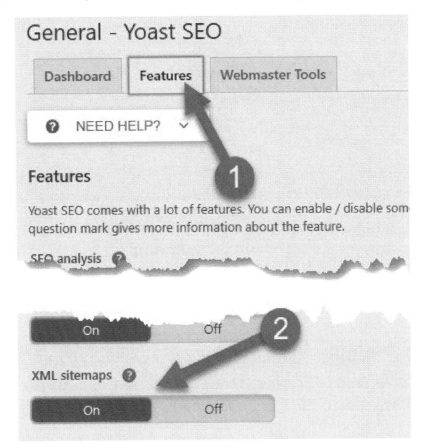

Scroll down to the **XML Sitemaps** listing. It is probably on by default, but make sure it is, then scroll to the bottom and save changes (even if you have not changed anything).

To see your sitemap, click the small "?" button next to the XML sitemap section and click the link to see the sitemap:

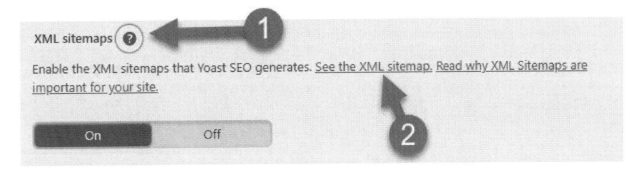

Click the link to be taken to your sitemap.

XML Sitemap

Generated by **YoastSEO**, this is an XML Sitemap, meant for consumption by search engines.

You can find more information about XML sitemaps on **sitemaps.org**.

This XML Sitemap Index file contains 4 sitemaps.

Sitemap	Last Modified
http://localhost/1hourwp/post-sitemap.xml	2018-11-06 10:48 +00:00
http://localhost/1hourwp/page-sitemap.xml	2018-11-06 10:37 +00:00
http://localhost/1hourwp/category-sitemap.xml	2018-11-06 10:48 +00:00
http://localhost/1hourwp/author-sitemap.xml	2018-11-06 13:36 +00:00

If you get a 404 error, meaning the page does not exist, make sure:

1. You have posts on your site that are published.
2. You have saved the permalink structure (even if you did not change it).

With a working sitemap, whenever you add a new post to your site it will automatically be added to this sitemap. Google and any other sites in your "ping list" will automatically be notified of the new content. You should find that once your site becomes established, new content will be indexed and found in Google within minutes of you clicking the "publish" button.

As we are getting close to adding content to the site, let's revisit posts and pages.

Pages v Posts

WordPress gives you two options for adding new content to your site. These are confusingly called "Pages" and "Posts".

Both use the exact same content editor, making it easy to add content. However, you need to decide which one, and when, to use each.

I've already hinted at when to use pages and when to use posts earlier in this book, but I'd like to revisit this topic and explain the differences between pages and posts.

From now on, whenever I talk about posts, I am referring to WordPress POSTS, and whenever I talk about pages, I am referring to WordPress PAGES.

WordPress was originally designed with bloggers in mind, and WordPress "posts" were the tool given to the blogger so they could add updates to the blog. These WordPress posts were designed to be date-dependent so that posts could be listed in chronological order. Think of it much like a diary. Things happen and you enter them in the order they happen. If you then ordered the posts in date order, with the oldest posts at the top, you'd have a chronological list of posts over time. This was how posts were originally designed to be used.

So, what about WordPress "pages"?

Well, pages are not date-dependent. They are standalone pages and each page is usually unrelated to any other piece of content on the site. Remember I said that "legal" pages should be pages? Can you see why?

Post Categories

A major difference between posts and pages is that posts can be grouped and categorized (reinforcing the idea that posts can be related to other posts), whereas pages cannot (this isn't strictly true, but it helps if you think it is).

Remember the website structure I mapped out earlier for a site about WordPress?

There were a number of related articles about various WordPress plugins. There were also a bunch of related articles reviewing WordPress themes. The beauty of grouping and categorizing content on your site is that WordPress makes it easy to manipulate these groups of posts and treat them as a related whole.

For example, if a visitor lands on my review of the Thesis WordPress theme, doesn't it make sense to show that visitor a list of other theme reviews to give them more information before they choose one to buy?

WordPress makes this easy with posts, but there is no easy, built-in way of doing this with WordPress pages. Pages were designed to be separate, standalone pieces of content, unrelated to anything else on the site.

All posts are given a category, whereas pages are not. Earlier in this book, I showed you the URL of the "Hello World!" post after we made the change to the permalink structure.

The word "Uncategorized" in the URL is the category of the post.

Uncategorized is a default category that WordPress added when it was installed. We can, and will, change that later. However, think about my fictional website. The URLs of my theme reviews might look like this:

http://illumnii.com/themes/thesis
http://illumnii.com/themes/avada
http://illumnii.com/themes/genesis
http://illumnii.com/themes/customizr-pro
http://illumnii.com/themes/hueman

Some of my plugin reviews might look like this:

```
http://illumnii.com/plugins/yarpp
http://illumnii.com/plugins/related-posts
http://illumnii.com/plugins/yoast-seo
http://illumnii.com/plugins/akismet
http://illumnii.com/plugins/wp-dbmanager
```

.. and so on. You can instantly see that these groups of posts are related, because of the category in the URL.

This is a major SEO (Search Engine Optimization) benefit of posts as well. The search engines see these posts in the same category, and this helps them categorize and rank your content. The search engines know that these groups of posts are related, and carefully selected categories will help them categorize and rank your pages accordingly.

WordPress actually helps out even more.

For every category you create (I have two in the examples above – themes and plugins), WordPress creates a "Category page" that lists all posts in that category. Therefore, there will be a category page for themes and another for plugins. Their URLs will be as follows:

```
http://illumnii.com/category/plugins/
http://illumnii.com/category/themes/
```

The first category page will list all posts in the plugin category, and the second will list all posts in the theme category.

The search engines know that WordPress category pages list related posts, so it automatically knows that all posts listed on a category page have a common theme.

So, we can assign categories to posts. In fact, a post can be given more than one category. However, I don't recommend it. Categories are the top level of organization of posts, and I want you to stick to only using ONE category per post. What would a search engine "think" if a post was in two categories? It would probably wonder what the post was about, category 1 or category 2.

However, what if I had a category called "reviews"?

My "theme" posts could then go into both the themes category and the reviews category.

Similarly, my plugin reviews could go into the plugin category AND the review category.

If you have this dilemma, then you probably need to re-assess your category structure. However, WordPress does give us another tool that can help solve the problem.

Tags!

Post Tags

So, categories are the main way we categorize and group posts. WordPress also gives us a secondary method for categorizing content, called Tags. These are just words or phrases we can assign to a post, like keywords related to the post. So, we could "tag" all review posts as "reviews", while keeping them in tightly focused categories.

Just as WordPress creates a "category page" for all categories you define, it also creates a tag page for each tag you use. For example, if you tagged 5 of your posts with the tag "review", then WordPress would create a review tag page that lists those five posts.

http://illumnii.com/tag/review/

On the reviews tag page of my WordPress site, we would see posts from both the themes and plugins categories. Can you see the power of this? It's an extra level of organization!

A post can have multiple tags assigned to it, but only create tags if they are going to be used on multiple posts. Never use a tag that will only appear in one post.

The rule is that each post should only be in ONE category, but can have multiple tags.

Let me give you an example of when you might use a tag.

Suppose you have a site about vacuum cleaners. You have decided on categories like Dyson, Hoover, Eureka, Kirby, Dirt Devil and so on. In other words, you are using the manufacturer names as categories. All Dyson vacuum reviews go in the Dyson category, all Kirby reviews go in the Kirby category.

This makes sense because as webmaster, you decided that most visitors know the brand of vacuum they want, so grouping by brand helps them more easily find the model that suits them best. To find a Dyson, they can simply go to your Dyson category page where all Dyson reviews are listed.

However, sometimes a visitor does not know the brand of vacuum he wants. All they know is that they want a hand-held vacuum, or a canister vacuum, or maybe a vacuum designed to deal with pet hair.

This is where I would use tags.

I'd have the following tags:

Upright, canister, pets, hand-held, HEPA filter, etc.

Therefore, my Dyson DC31 Animal review would be put in the Dyson category, but I could tag it with pets and hand-held.

The beauty of tags is that we can manipulate them in the same way we do categories. If someone on your site is interested in a "hand-held vacuums", but not sure which manufacturer, you can show them a list of all vacuums "tagged" with "hand-held".

As mentioned earlier, WordPress creates a "tag page" for each tag you use. Each tag page lists all posts that have used that tag. So WordPress would create a page that lists all "hand-held" vacuum reviews.

Sound familiar? Yes, it's very much like the category pages we mentioned earlier.

So, posts can have categories and tags assigned to them.

I do have a few rules on using categories and tags efficiently. These rules will keep you out of trouble. Here they are:

1. Only one category per post.
2. You can have multiple tags, but try to limit each post to 5 or fewer tags. The more tags you use in a post, the more spammy your site begins to look to Google.
3. Never use a tag if only one post will be tagged with it. I personally only create a tag if it will be used on a minimum of three posts. Tags, like categories, are there to help organize and group your posts. If there is only one post using a tag, it's not a group. Remember that WordPress creates a "tag page" for each tag you use. If you only have one post using a tag, then that tag page will basically just contain one post. That would be considered duplicate content by Google since you already have that one post on its own "post page", as well as on a category page.
4. Never create a tag with the same name as a category.

Tags are ultimately there to help you make your site better for your visitors. Don't abuse them.

Post Excerpts

Another great feature is post **excerpts.** When you enter a post, you have the option of entering an excerpt as well.

If you are using the Classic editor for posts and pages, you have one step you need to complete first. That is because by default, WordPress hides the excerpt entry box on the edit post screen, so we need to unhide it. To hide and unhide various aspects of the Dashboard, WordPress has "Screen Options", which you can see in the top right of your dashboard (you won't see this if you are using the Gutenberg editor).

The screen options you see at any point in the dashboard will be related to the section of the dashboard you are currently viewing. Therefore, since excerpts are related to posts, we need to be adding or editing a post to see the option.

Click on **Posts** in the sidebar menu. This will bring up a list of posts on your site. If you have one, click on the title of the post to open the editing screen. If you don't have one, click **Add New** (in the posts menu). This will create a post and open it for editing.

Now that you are on the post editing screen, click where it says "Screen Options" to open the menu:

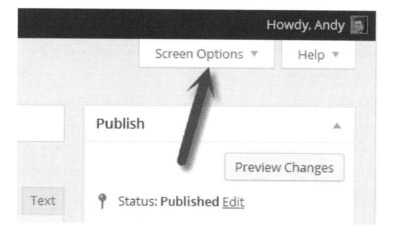

Clicking that button will expand it:

As you can see, **Excerpt** is unchecked. If we check that box, the Edit post screen adds this new entry box:

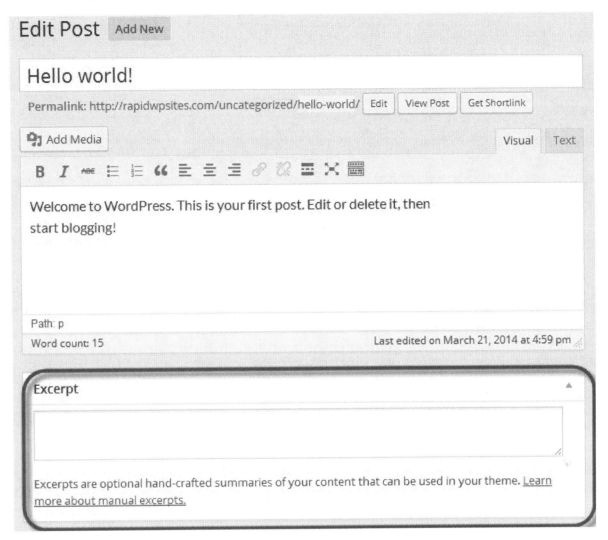

Now when I enter a post, I can also enter a separate excerpt.

Note that the "Screen Options" are dynamic, and will show you just the options that are relevant to the Dashboard screen you are viewing. In the screenshots above, I am in the Edit post screen, so the options I am given relate to the Edit posts screen.

No Screen Options in Gutenberg Editor

If you are using the Gutenberg editor you won't have the screen options on the edit post/page screen. The excerpt box is there on the right-hand side of the editor:

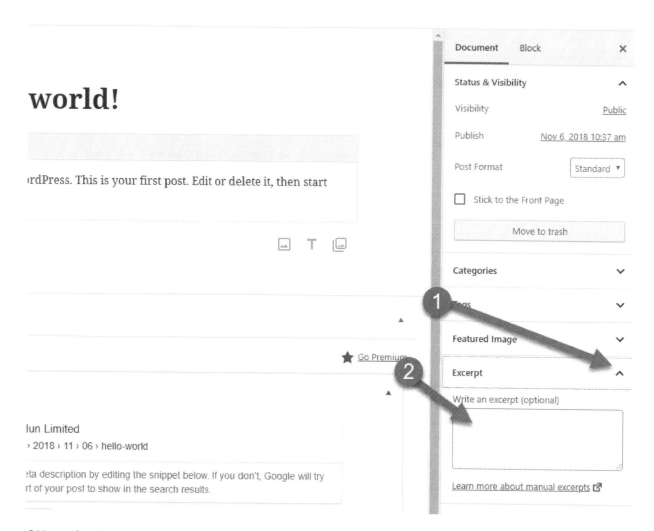

OK, so let's go back to our discussion of excerpts, and look at what they are, and why we would use them.

An excerpt is a short summary or description of a post. Some WordPress themes and plugins can use the excerpt, for example, to show to visitors, or as a meta description of the post.

Let's see an example of an excerpt being used properly on a site. This screenshot shows the sidebar of a website that is using a plugin to display recent posts in a category:

Juicing recipes

Very Berry Sprouted Smoothie

Alfalfa sprouts are a product of alfalfa seeds. The tiny sprouts are thread-like in structure with green tops. The seeds can be cultivated anywhere on the planet irrespective of climate or temperature. The highly nutritive sprouts have a mild taste making them the ideal addition to any smoothie recipe.

Paleo Tomato Salad

Enthusiasts of paleo and primal diets love this recipe: Ingredients: 3 or 4 tomatoes Bacon lardons 2 boiled eggs A tablespoon of mayonnaise A few anchovies A tablespoon of olive oil. Directions: Combine the sliced tomatoes with peeled boiled eggs cut into squares in a large salad bowl. Fry the bacon, let it cool and [...]

Notice the top one. The description of the post is nicely defined and "complete". The one lower down, however, is not. Notice that the description for the second one ends with [...].

This plugin looks for an excerpt to use as the post description. If it finds an excerpt, it will use it. If it does not find one, it will use the first bit of text in the article and create a description from that. When it does that, you end up with a description that is not complete, copied from the start of the article, and ends with [...].

You can see how using excerpts makes your site look more professional, and better for your visitors. It also allows you to write some unique text that will act as a description to entice visitors. It's also better for the search engines because they see different content in the description, instead of just part of the first paragraph of the post.

Posts and RSS Feeds

Another important difference between posts and pages is that posts appear in RSS feeds, pages do not.

WordPress sites automatically create RSS feeds. These are special files that contain a list of the most recent posts on your site.

WordPress creates a single RSS feed for your entire site, but it also creates separate feeds for each category, each tag, all posts by a particular author, etc.

RSS feeds are important tools to notify people, and other websites, that you have published new content. Personally, I monitor the RSS feeds (using a free service over at Feedly.com) of my favorite websites, and when they post new content, the feed is updated (automatically by WordPress) and I get notified of that new content.

When to Use Posts and When to Use Pages

OK, this is the million-dollar question that I get asked a lot!

This will depend on the type of website you want to build and we will mention this again later in the book when we discuss website structure again.

For a lot of company websites, using pages for most of the content makes sense, like this:

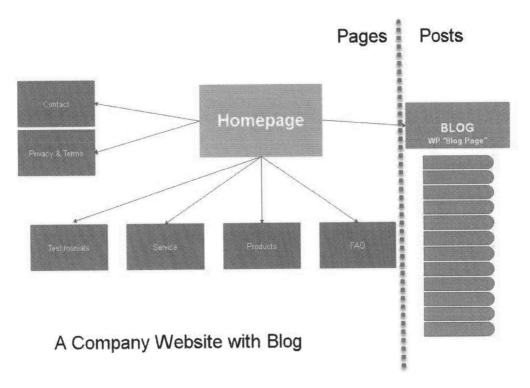

A Company Website with Blog

Everything to the left of the dotted line is a Page. Everything to the right is a Post.

In this model, the company site uses WordPress "pages" for all of the main important content that they want to convey to visitors. So homepage, contact, legal pages, testimonials, services, products, and FAQ. These pieces of content are all isolated and unrelated to the other pages. And that is where a page comes in useful.

The company site also has a blog, and in this model, the blog is built with posts. From the point of view of this company, what features of posts make them ideal for the blog?

The main type of website I personally build uses a different model. It is a model that particularly suites niche sites, eCommerce, etc. It's a model that relies on the fact that a piece of content does not live on an island, it is related to other pieces of content, which can be grouped and categorized.

This model offers great SEO benefits as well as organizing content in a logical manner to help both visitors and search engines. Before I tell you the model, let me first distinguish between two types of content that you may have on your site.

The first type of content is your "call to action" stuff. It's the content you want your visitors to see. The content you want ranking high in Google. We will call this type of content, **Niche Content**. This will include articles, reviews, videos, infographics, etc. that **you create for your site and your targeted audience**.

The second type of content is the stuff that you need to have on the site, but from a financial point of view, you don't really care whether visitors find it. This type of content does not fit into logical groups as we saw with posts. Typical examples would be a Privacy page and Terms of Service. I'd also add the "contact" and "about us" pages to this grouping. I call this type of content my "legal pages".

Do you understand the difference? Here is the basic rule I used in this website model.

Use Posts for "Niche Content", and Pages for "Legal Pages".

Here is a diagram of the model:

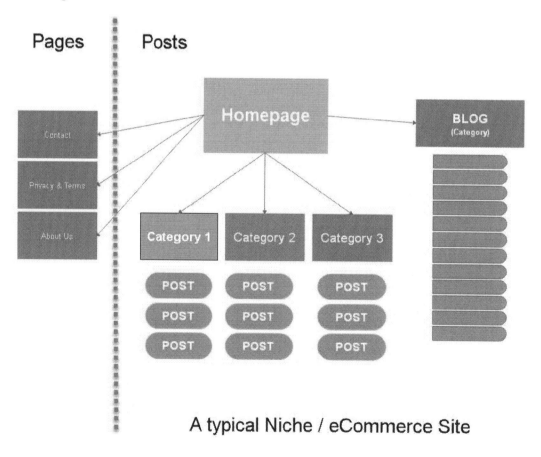

A typical Niche / eCommerce Site

On the left of the dotted line, you can see the pages. On the right (with the exception of the homepage), all content you create uses WordPress posts.

It's a simple enough rule, and it will make perfect sense when we start adding pages and posts to the website. Before we can do that though, we need to look at how we write posts.

Writing Posts

As you know, WordPress 5.0 changed the way we write content from the classic WYSIWYG editor to the new Gutenberg editor. Depending on what version of WordPress you are using and even which plugins you have installed, you may be using one, other, or both, editors. Don't panic. I will cover both editors here, so you know the main differences, then the choice is yours.

If you are using WordPress 5.x and Gutenberg is the only editor you have, then you can install the Classic editor as a plugin if you wish. Install and activate this plugin:

If you are using WordPress version 4.x, you can install Gutenberg as a plugin. Install and activate this plugin:

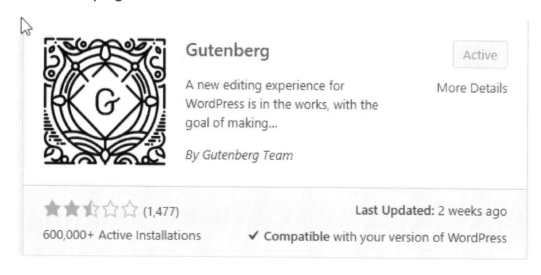

Choosing the Classic Editor or Gutenberg

To recap...

If you want to use Gutenberg, then don't install the Classic Editor plugin. All posts and pages will then be created in the Gutenberg editor.

If you want to use the classic editor and you are using the Gutenberg enabled WordPress 5.x, install and activate the plugin. All add post and page links will then default to the Classic editor.

With that said, let's look at how you can add content, first using the Classic editor, then using Gutenberg.

The Classic Editor

To create a new post on your site, click **Add New** in the **Posts** menu.

The **Add New Post** (and **Add New Page**) screen has a lot of information on it. Let's look at the **What You See Is What You Get (WYSIWYG)** Editor first.

Adding a Post With the "Classic" WYSIWYG Editor

The toolbar of the editor (the place where you add your content), looks like this:

If you only see one line of buttons on your toolbar, click the **Toggle Toolbar** button on the right. That will expand the toolbar.

You'll see on the top right there are two tabs – **Visual** & **Text**.

The Visual tab is where you can write your content using WYSIWYG features. On this tab, you'll see text and media formatted as it will appear on the website once published. This is the tab you will want to use for most of the work you do when adding new, or editing existing content, on your site.

The other tab – Text – shows the raw code that is responsible for the layout and content of the page. Unless you specifically need to insert some code or script into your content, stick with the Visual tab.

The two rows of buttons allow you to format your content visually. If you have used any type of Word Processor before, then this should be intuitive.

I won't go through the functions of all these buttons. If you need help understanding what a button does, move your mouse over it to get a popup help tooltip.

Adding content to your site is as easy as typing it into the large box under the toolbar. Just use it like you would any word processor.

Write your content. Select some text and click a formatting button to apply the format. Make it bold, or change its color, make it a header, or any of the other features offered in the toolbar.

To create a headline, enter the headline and press the return button on your keyboard to make sure it is on its own line. Now click somewhere in the headline and select the headline from the drop-down box in the toolbar.

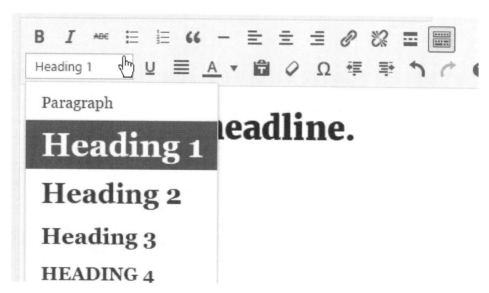

NOTE: WordPress themes typically show the title of your post as an H1 header at the top of the page. This is the biggest header available and is equivalent to the **Heading1** in the drop-down selector. You should not use more than one H1 header on a web page, so avoid using **Heading 1** as you write your content. Use **Heading 2** for main sections within your article, and **Heading 3** for sub-headers inside **Heading 2** sections.

OK, it's now time to go ahead and write the post for your website.

As you write your article, you may want to insert an image or some other form of media. We looked at the Media library earlier in the book, but let's go through the process of adding an image to an article.

Adding Images

The process is straightforward.

Position your cursor in the article where you want to add the image. Don't worry too much about getting it in the right place because you can always re-position it later if you need to.

Click the **Add Media** button located above the WYSIWYG editor, to the left, and you'll see the popup screen that we've seen previously:

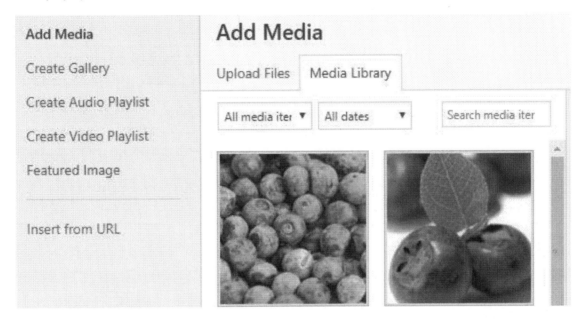

From this screen, you can select an image from the media library, or click the **Upload Files** tab to upload a new image to the media library.

Let's add an image from our Media Library.

Click the **Media Library** tab if it is not already selected and click on the image you want to use in the post.

A check mark appears in the top right corner of the image, and the "attachment" details are displayed on the right side. These image details can be edited if you want to.

At the bottom of the right sidebar is an **Insert into post** button. Before you click that, we should consider a few of the sidebar options.

One important option is the **Alt Text**. This text is read to the visually impaired visitors on your site and helps them understand what images are being shown. Therefore, add a short descriptive ALT text. For my example, **blueberries** is sufficient.

At the bottom of the right-hand column are some **Attachment Display Settings**. Currently, my image is set to "none" for alignment.

I want to align the image to the left so can select that from the drop-down box. When an image is aligned left (or right) in WordPress, the post text wraps around it. If you select **None** or **Center** for alignment, the text won't wrap.

The next option you have is to link your image to something. The default setting is **None**, meaning we insert an image that is not clickable by the visitor because it is not linked to anything. This is the setting I use on 99% of all images I embed in posts.

You can link an image to a **Media File**, **Attachment page** or **Custom URL**.

The one that I think you will find the most useful is the **Custom** URL. This allows you to navigate to a URL when a user clicks an image. For example, if your image is a "Buy Now" button, you'd want the image linked to the purchase page.

The last of the display settings is **Size**. You'll be able to choose from **Full size** and **thumbnail**. The dimensions are included with each file size, so choose the one that is closest to the size you want the image to appear on your page.

I want my image to be full-sized (as I had resized the image to the correct size before I uploaded it to the media library), so I'd select **Full Size**.

Once you have made your selection, click the **Insert into post** button at the bottom.

Here is that image inserted into my post at the position of my cursor:

condimentum gravida. Nunc finibus risus et bibendum
cursus. Ut ut libero vitae odio hendrerit varius sed eu
tortor.

Fusce malesuada
aliquam dolor, eu
sagittis elit cursus
nec. Etiam nec
dictum ante. Vivamus
tempor finibus
ipsum, ac elementum
diam facilisis nec.
Nulla laoreet ex a
ullamcorper eleifend. Sed fermentum velit dui, eget
semper nulla fermentum vel. Nunc id sagittis mauris, non

If you have the position wrong, you can simply click the image to select it, and drag the image to a different location.

If you find that the image isn't inserted as you intended (e.g. you forgot to align it), click on the image. A toolbar appears above the image and a bounding box around it:

The bounding box includes a small square in each corner. You can use this to resize the image. Drag one of the corners to make the image bigger or smaller.

The first 4 buttons in the toolbar allow you to re-align the image.

The last button in the toolbar will delete the image.

The toolbar edit button looks like a pencil. You can use this to open the **Image Details** screen to make a number of changes:

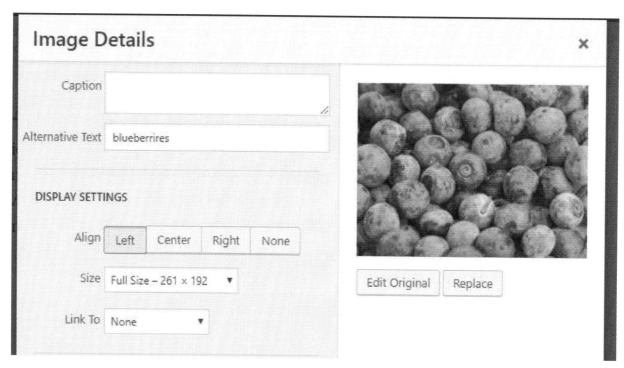

You'll also see a link to **Advanced Options** at the bottom. Click that to expand the advanced options:

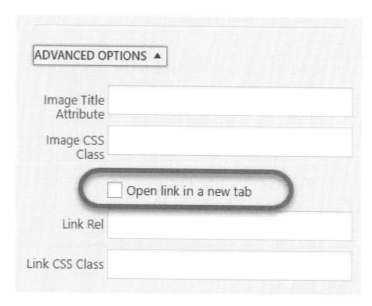

The advanced option that is most useful to us is the **Open link in a new tab** option. When someone clicks the image, whatever it is linked to opens in a new browser tab.

Once you have made your edits on this screen, click the **Update** button and the changes will be updated in your post.

You can insert videos from your Media library in the same way.

OK, finish your first post.

Something to try: We added an image that was already in the Media Library. Go ahead and add an image from your hard disk. After clicking the Add Media button, you'll need to go to the Upload tab to proceed. Try it and see if you can successfully add an image this way.

Once you've done that, try adding an image to a post by dragging and dropping the image from your computer directly into the WYSIWYG editor window.

It's all very intuitive.

There are a few things we need to do before we publish a post, so let's go through the complete sequence from start, to publish:

1. Add a post title.
2. Write & format your post using the visual text editor (WYSIWYG).
3. Select a post format if available. You can ignore this option for most posts you add.
4. Select a category.
5. Add some tags if you want to. Tags can always be added later, so don't feel under any pressure to add them now. Of course, you can also decide you don't want to use tags on your site. That is fine too.
6. Add an excerpt.
7. Select a date/time if you want to schedule the post for the future.
8. Publish/Schedule the post.

OK, we have completed down to step 2.

Post Formats

Not all WordPress themes use "Post Formats". The Twenty Sixteen theme that we are using does and you can see them on the right of your screen:

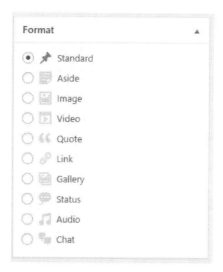

Since most, if not all your posts, should use the default (Standard), we won't go into details in this book about other formats. Most people just won't use them and not all themes support them.

If you are interested in post formats, experiment with them. Select one and update your post. Then view your post to see how it looks. You can also read more about Post Formats on the WordPress websites:

http://codex.WordPress.org/Post_Formats

Post Category

The next step in our publishing sequence is to choose a category. Choose just one category for each post.

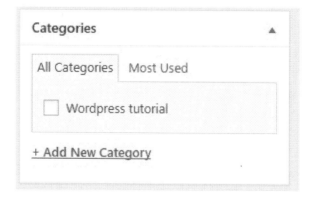

If you forget to check a category box, WordPress will automatically use your default category.

You can add a new category "on the fly" from within the **Add post** screen, but if you do, remember to go in and write a description for the new category so it can be used as the meta description of that category page (remember the Yoast SEO plugin we set up earlier is expecting a description of categories and tags).

Post Tags

If you want to use tags for the post, you can type them directly into the tags box, even if they don't already exist. When you are finished typing the tags, click the **Add** button to the right of the tags box.

As you add and use more tags, you can click on the link **Choose from the most used tags** and a box will appear with some of the tags you've used before. You can just click the tags that apply and they'll be added to the tag list of your post.

If you add new tags when entering a post, remember to go into the Tags settings to write a short description for each one. Yes, it takes time. However, this will be used as the Meta description of the tag page.

Post Excerpt

You should add a post excerpt to all posts. If you don't see an excerpt entry box on your screen, check the **Screen Options** to make sure **Excerpt** is checked.

Once checked, the **Excerpt** box magically appears on your edit post screen.

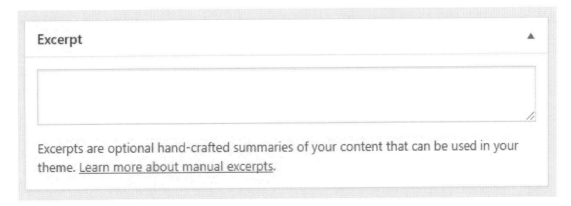

The excerpt should be a short description of the post you are writing. Its purpose is to encourage visitors to click through and read the article (e.g. From the search engine).

This excerpt will be used as the Meta description tag of the post, as well as the description of the post in the "related posts" section, which is displayed at the end of each article you publish (see the YARPP plugin later).

Enter a three to five sentence excerpt that encourages the click.

Publishing the Post

The next step in the process is deciding when you want the post to go live on your site. Let's look at the **Publish** section of the screen.

The first option you have is to save the post as a draft.

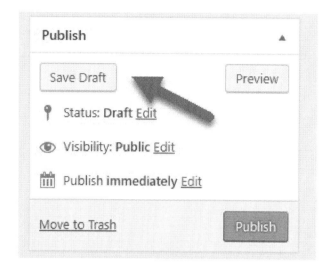

Once saved as a draft, you can go back at any time to make changes or publish the article. Draft posts are not shown on your site. To be visible on your website, you need to publish the post.

If you want it up there immediately, then click the Publish button. If like me, you are writing several posts in a batch, it is a good idea to spread the posting of the content out a little bit. Luckily, WordPress allows us to schedule the posts into the future.

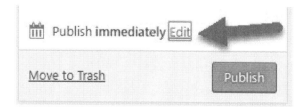

The default is to publish **immediately**. However, there is an **Edit** link you can click to open a scheduling calendar:

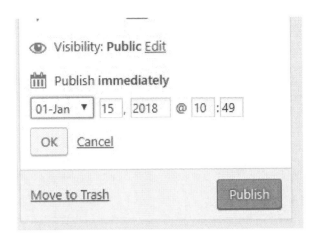

Enter the date and time you want to publish the post and then click the OK button.

The publish button now changes to **Schedule**.

Click the **Schedule** button to schedule the post.

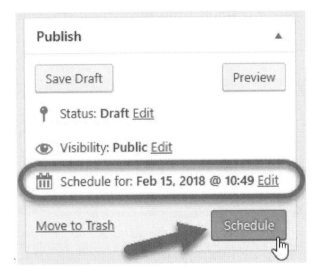

That's it. You've just published or scheduled your first WordPress post using the Classic editor.

Adding a Post with the Gutenberg Editor

If you've ever used a WordPress "page builder" like Elementor, then Gutenberg will seem a lot more familiar to you. You see, like other page builders, Gutenberg uses a system of blocks to help you build your content. On adding a new post or page, you'll be greeted with the Gutenberg editor:

There are two simple prompts: **Add title** and **Write your story**.

If you move your mouse over the "Add Title" text, a box appears:

Click into that box, and you can type the title of your post.

Now move your mouse over the "Write your story" text. This area becomes active, and you see a + symbol in a circle on the left, and a set of three icons on the right:

These are the new controls for adding content to your post.

When you click the + button, a menu appears offering you a number of different blocks you can add to your post:

The search box at the top makes it easy to find the block you want, but that will become more useful as you learn what is available. This menu is the main way to add new blocks, but not the only way. Remember the buttons on the right?

Omega-3 Rich Krill Oil

These buttons can add different types of blocks to your post. But be aware that the exact buttons offered may not be the same as the ones in my screenshot (see later). The ones I have there are:

1. shortcode (as we saw earlier in the book when adding a shortcode for our contact form),
2. image, and
3. heading.

With Gutenberg, you build your web pages using blocks.

In its simplest form, a post could be simply a title and a **paragraph** block, like this:

Omega-3 Rich Krill Oil

We buy krill oil supplements mostly for their omega-3 content. Your body needs omega-3 to perform a whole range of bodily functions, making it one of the most vital nutrients to supplement with today. The reason why a lot of people need omega-3 in supplement form is because it's one of the nutrients that's lacking in the typical western diet. Krill oil supplements can benefit human health in the following areas:

Note that there is only one paragraph per block. If you are writing a block of text, and press the Enter key to start a new paragraph, Gutenberg will automatically create a new paragraph block for the second paragraph. In the following screenshot, I pressed the Enter key after the colon:

Omega-3 Rich Krill Oil

We buy krill oil supplements mostly for their omega-3 content. Your body needs omega-3 to perform a whole range of bodily functions, making it one of the most vital nutrients to supplement with today. The reason why a lot of people need omega-3 in supplement form is because it's one of the nutrients that's lacking in the typical western diet. Krill oil supplements can benefit human health in the following areas:

Can you see that Gutenberg automatically created a new paragraph block? Go on and try it for yourself. Note that I now have different buttons on the right. The **heading** button I had in the previous screenshot is now replaced by a **list item** button. That is because I was recently working on a list item block, so Gutenberg thinks it is more relevant to me. We'll see it change again in a moment.

This auto-addition of new paragraph blocks makes writing long pieces of content very easy because you do not need to manually create paragraph blocks as you type.

If you tend to write your content in an external editor and then paste it into WordPress, if you are pasting several paragraphs into a paragraph block, you'll find that Gutenberg automatically splits the text into multiple paragraph blocks for you!

The advantage of using one block per paragraph is that each paragraph can then be treated differently, e.g. in terms of formatting.

Paragraph Block Properties

All blocks have their own properties. Since we've added a paragraph block, let's check out the properties because you can do some interesting stuff. Click into a paragraph block. On the right-hand side, you should see the **Block** tab has been selected:

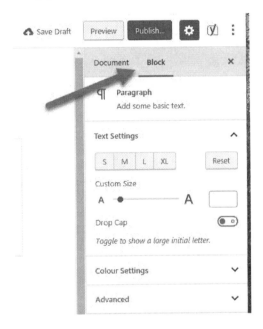

The **Block** tab shows you the settings for that block only (as opposed to the **Document** tab which has settings affecting the entire document). You can see buttons for text size - small, medium, large and extra-large, plus a slider and edit box for more precise control of font size. Go on and try these settings out.

The **Drop Cap** option can add some interest to your paragraph:

Omega-3 Rich Krill Oil

¶▾ ☰ ☰ ☰ **B** *I* 🔗 ᴀʙᴇ ⋮

We buy krill oil supplements mostly for their omega-3 content. Your body needs omega-3 to perform a whole range of bodily functions, making it one of the most vital nutrients to supplement with today. The reason why a lot of people need omega-3 in supplement form is because it's one of the nutrients that's lacking in the typical western diet. Krill oil supplements can benefit human health in the following areas:

The paragraph block also has **Color Settings** that allow you to define the text and background color.

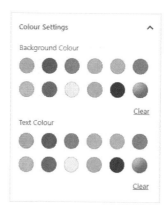

This gives you more flexibility in how your text appears on the page:

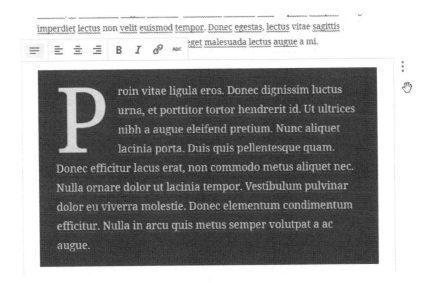

imperdiet lectus non velit euismod tempor. Donec egestas, lectus vitae sagittis
eget malesuada lectus augue a mi.

You will also find further formatting options in a toolbar at the top of the selected
block. The formatting options available will obviously depend on the type of block you
have selected. For a paragraph block:

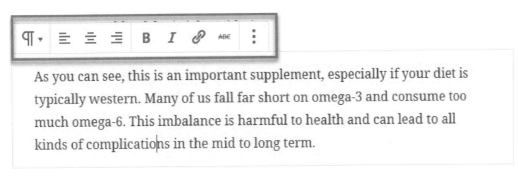

The first button that shows a paragraph symbol indicates the block type. In this case a
paragraph ☺. However, clicking that button allows you to convert the block type to
a "compatible" alternative. Paragraph blocks can be converted to:

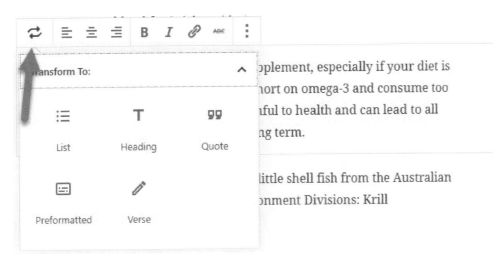

The other options include alignment, bold, italic, link & strikethrough. The alignment will affect the whole paragraph, but the other 4 buttons will only be applied to the selected text within the paragraph:

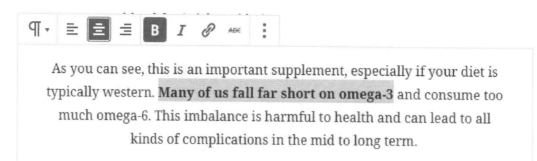

The final menu button in the toolbar gives you a few block-related options:

So, you can duplicate the block, insert a block before or after the current one, edit as HTML and add the block to "Reusable Blocks".

Reusable Blocks

These are an interesting feature. It means you can save a block to be reused across your site. If you update the reusable block, you update it everywhere you use it.

To make a block reusable, click inside the block you want to use, and click the menu button. Select **Add to Reusable Blocks.**

You'll be prompted for a name:

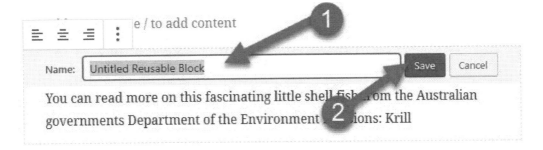

Enter a name for the reusable block and save.

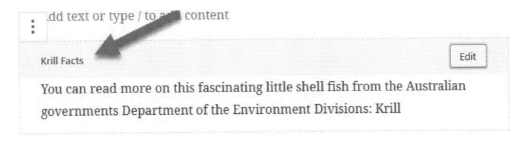

I called mine **Krill Facts**. Once saved, the reusable block will appear in the block list:

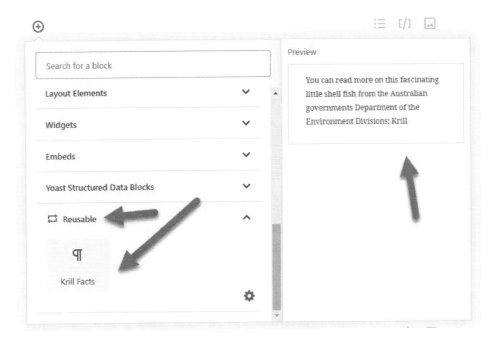

If you mouseover a reusable block, you get a preview on the right.

Adding an Image Block

There are a few ways we can add an image to our post.

Firstly, we can move our mouse towards the top of the paragraph block until we see a "+" appear in the middle of the block:

omega-3 in supplement form is because it's one of the nutrients that's lacking in the typical western diet. Krill oil supplements can benefit human health i[Insert block]wing areas:

Paragraph

As you can see, this is an important supplement, especially if your diet is typically western. Many of us fall far short on omega-3 and consume too much omega-6. This imbalance is harmful to health and can lead to all kinds of complications in the mid to long term.

Clicking that would create a new empty block above the current paragraph block:

supplement with today. The reason why a lot of people need omega-3 in supplement form is because it's one of the nutrients that's lacking in the typical western diet. Krill oil supplements can benefit human health in the following areas:

As you can see, this is an important supplement, especially if your diet is typically western. Many of us fall far short on omega-3 and consume too much omega-6. This imbalance is harmful to health and can lead to all kinds of complications in the mid to long term.

I can then either click the "+" button on the left and select image or click the image button in the right-hand toolbar. Both will achieve the same thing:

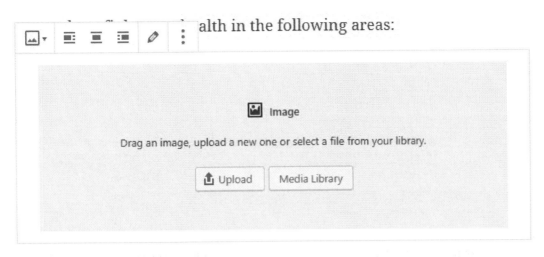

alth in the following areas:

As you can see, this is an important supplement, especially if your diet is

The image block is inserted. As you can see, you can upload an image, drag and drop an image over the block, or choose an image from the Media Library. All of the options will insert the image into the block:

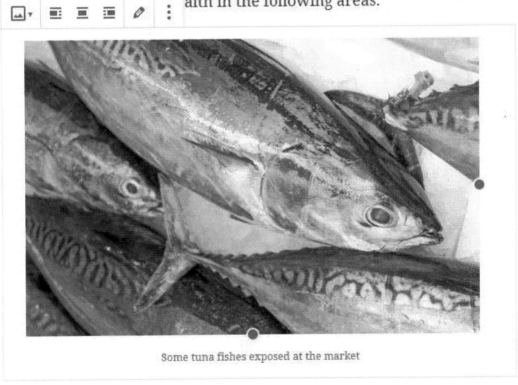

that's lacking in the typical western diet. Krill oil supplements

alth in the following areas:

Some tuna fishes exposed at the market

As you can see, this is an important supplement, especially if your diet is typically western. Many of us fall far short on omega-3 and consume too

You'll see some editing buttons across the top left. You have the usual convert block button, plus alignment and the block menu. You also have the edit button which you can use to select a different image.

You'll also notice a caption underneath the image. Click into the caption to edit, or delete it altogether.

At the moment, the image is sitting above the text. If I want the text to flow around the image, I can select the left align button in the toolbar, and then use the bounding box handles on the image to resize the image accordingly:

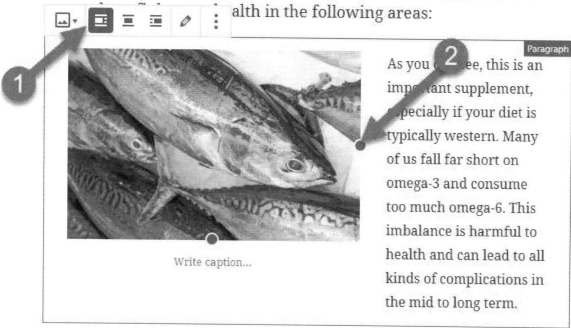

omega-3 in supplement form is because it's one of the nutrients that's lacking in the typical western diet. Krill oil supplements ... alth in the following areas:

As you can see, this is an important supplement, especially if your diet is typically western. Many of us fall far short on omega-3 and consume too much omega-6. This imbalance is harmful to health and can lead to all kinds of complications in the mid to long term.

Write caption...

You can read more on this fascinating little shell fish from the Australian governments Department of the Environment Divisions: Krill

Do you remember I said there were a few ways to add the image block?

The second way is to click the "+" in the top left of the editor screen:

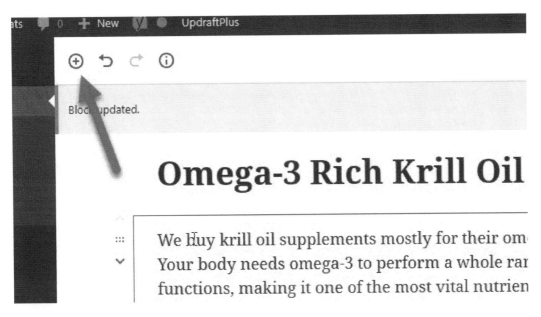

You'll be asked to choose which block you want to add, and on selecting a block type, it will be inserted into your post after the currently selected block.

e.g. If I have clicked into the first paragraph on the page, and then inserted a block in this manner, the new block will be inserted after the first paragraph.

Moving a Block in Gutenberg

Move your mouse to the inside left of the block you want to move. Two arrows appear allowing you to move the block up or down one position:

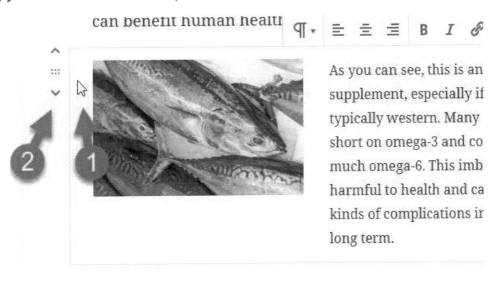

Try this...

Add an image block, then align left and wrap text as I have done. Now move your mouse inside left of the block containing the image. Try to move it down (or up).

Notice the image does not move but the text does. The clue is in the first button of the toolbar when you move your mouse inside left:

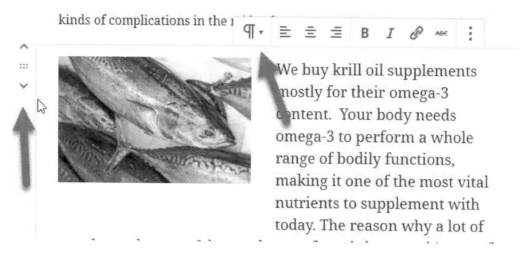

It's a paragraph block. Therefore, the paragraph block is the one that is moved.

To move the image, make sure you actually have the image block selected:

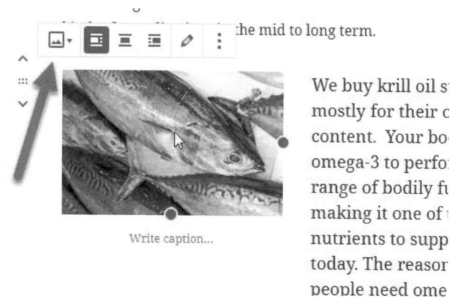

So, we've looked at adding images and moving them around. But what about all of the image properties like ALT text, size, linking the image to something, etc. How do you access those properties?

Remember earlier when we looked at the block properties of a paragraph block? That gave you access to the properties of the paragraph.

To access the properties of an image, select the image block and you'll see the image properties on the right:

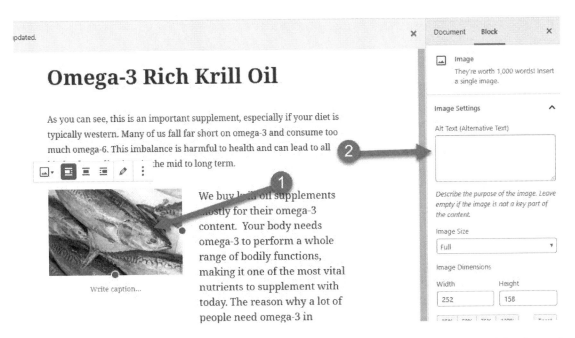

Omega-3 Rich Krill Oil

As you can see, this is an important supplement, especially if your diet is typically western. Many of us fall far short on omega-3 and consume too much omega-6. This imbalance is harmful to health and can lead to all ...he mid to long term.

We buy krill oil supplements ...ostly for their omega-3 content. Your body needs omega-3 to perform a whole range of bodily functions, making it one of the most vital nutrients to supplement with today. The reason why a lot of people need omega-3 in

Write caption...

To access the properties of any item (block) on your page, select the block and the block settings on the right will change to reflect the options for that block type.

Inserting Blocks in Between Existing Blocks

Each block in your post will display the toolbar at the top when you click into it. The right-hand button is the menu button that gives you the opportunity to insert a block before, or after, the current one.

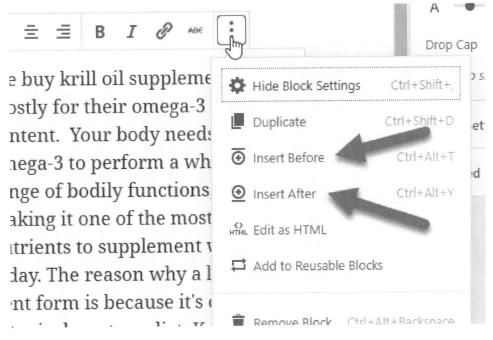

These options will insert a blank block which you can then work with:

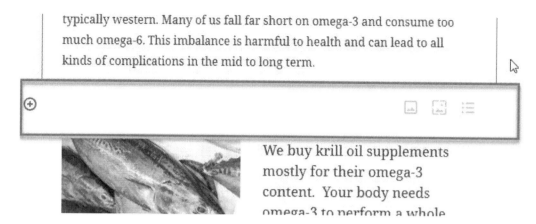

typically western. Many of us fall far short on omega-3 and consume too much omega-6. This imbalance is harmful to health and can lead to all kinds of complications in the mid to long term.

We buy krill oil supplements mostly for their omega-3 content. Your body needs omega-3 to perform a whole

Also, note that there are keyboard shortcuts for some items in the menu. For example, if you want to insert a block before an existing block, click the block and use the keyboard shortcut Ctrl+Alt+T (or the Mac equivalent).

We have already seen another way to insert one block between two others. Move your mouse over the top middle of the lower block and click the "+" to insert the block above:

today. The reason why a lot of people need omega-3 in supplement form is because it's one of the nutrients that's lacking in the typical western diet. Krill oil supplements can benefit human health in the following areas:

You can read more on this fascinating little shell fish from the Australian governments Department of the Environment Divisions: Krill

To Delete a Block

Deleting a block is easy too. Choose **Remove Block** from the menu on the right of the block:

Alternatively, you can use the Ctrl+Alt+Bksp keyboard shortcut as shown in the screenshot above.

So, we have the basics of adding blocks. What blocks are actually available?

Available "Building" Blocks

The blocks menu is divided into groups of related blocks:

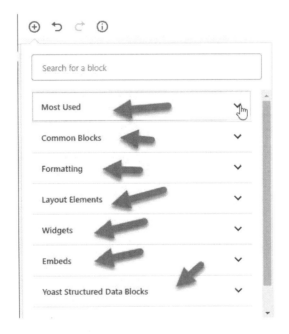

Just click the arrow on the right to unfold each set.

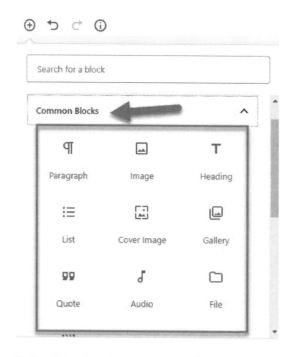

I won't go through all of the blocks that are available, but these are the ones you'll probably find yourself using regularly.

- Paragraph
- Image
- Heading
- List
- Quote
- Video
- Audio
- Table
- Button
- Columns
- Separator
- Spacer

I won't go through what each of these blocks actually does. You can try them out and see for yourself. Explore the blocks available to you. Add a block and then check out the block settings on the right of the Gutenberg editor.

There are a couple of blocks I would like to pay special attention to.

One that is well-overdue for WordPress users is the table block. It's found in the formatting section, but it is easier to just search for it:

When you add a table block, you'll be asked for the row and column count. You can always edit this later by adding new columns or rows, but it is easier if you know now and can enter the precise dimensions.

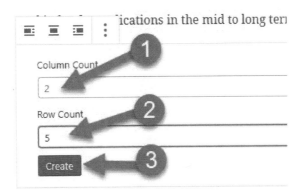

On clicking **Create**, you'll have a nicely formatted table awaiting data.

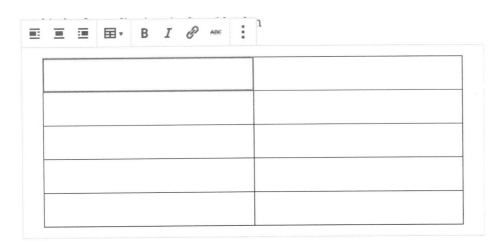

Now you can easily add properly formatted tables to your content:

Look at the toolbar that you get with a table block.

Those icons should all be familiar, with the exception of the 4th button, which includes a little downward facing arrow. That arrow means there is a menu attached to that button:

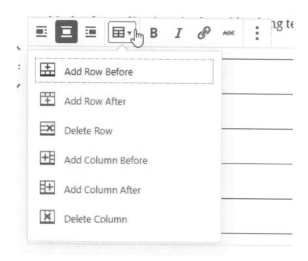

You can explore these for yourself. Create a table and try adding data to it. Insert columns and rows to the table. Then delete extra columns and rows until you are comfortable working with tables. Have a look at the table block properties.

Another cool block is the **Button** block.

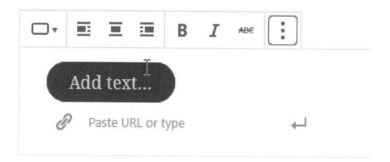

Insert a button block and click onto the text of the button (that says **Add text...**). Now type a caption for your button. You can also specify a URL to link the button to. Do you want to take your visitor to the "hello world" post when they click it? Simply start typing in some text from the title of the post you want to link to, and it should pop up for you to select:

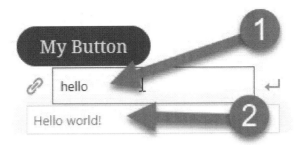

Select it and the URL of that post will be added to the URL box:

Click the little icon on the right to apply changes.

If you want the button to go to a webpage that is not part of your site, you can paste the URL directly into the URL box.

OK, with button created, select it and explore the toolbar. What can you transform it into?

Take a look at the properties of the button block:

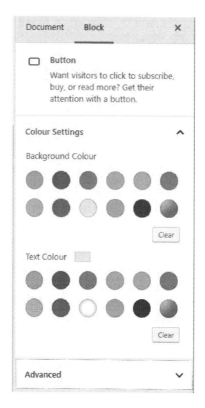

This block allows you to insert a button into your post, and style it as you like.

One other block that is nice to see is the columns block. This allows you to create sections of content that are divided into columns:

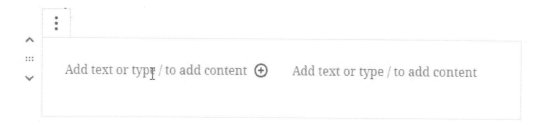

When you have the columns block selected, mousing over a column will add the + button. This lets you add blocks to each column separately.

Here is a two-column block that has an image (with caption) on the left, and a table on the right:

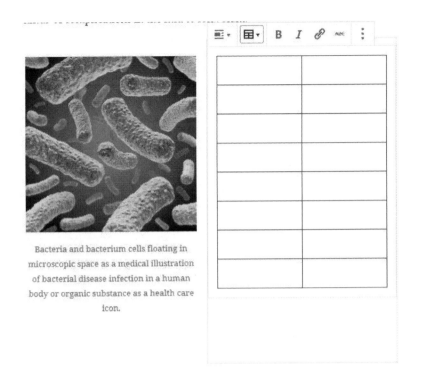

Bacteria and bacterium cells floating in microscopic space as a medical illustration of bacterial disease infection in a human body or organic substance as a health care icon.

That's quite cool!

Post (Document) Properties

As you work on your post or page, you have access to the document properties on the right.

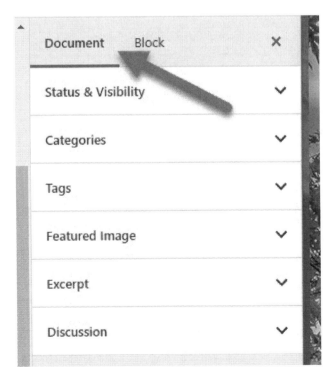

These settings allow you to set the category of a post, add tags, set a featured image, create an excerpt, etc.

The Process for Publishing a Post

When you are creating a post, you'll need to select the category of the post:

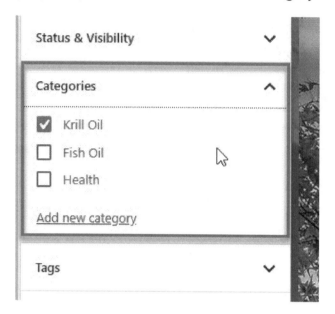

Notice that you can **Add a New Category** from the category settings if you need to. If you do add a category here, remember to go into the **Posts, Categories** settings to add a description for the new category.

You'll also need to decide if you want to add any tags:

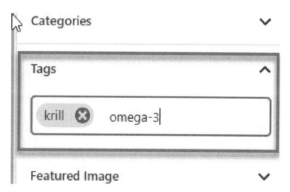

Just type them in, and press Enter on your keyboard. Try it!

You'll also need to select a featured image if you use one. These are small thumbnail images that can be used by your website's theme to display on your website. Google can also use these, so I advise you do include a featured image on all posts. When you have selected one, it will appear in this section of the Document settings:

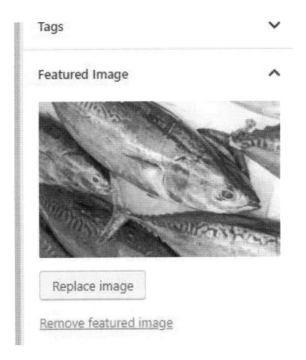

It is also a good idea to create an excerpt for all posts. This can be used by your site theme and Google to display a short description of the post.

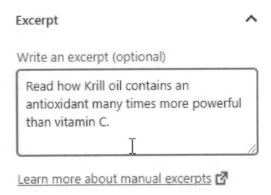

The last option in the document settings is the **Discussion** settings. This allows you to override default settings for posts:

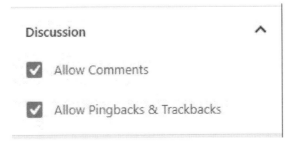

If I did not want to allow comments on a post, I could turn them off here.

The only option we have not covered in the document settings is the **Status & Visibility**. Let's do that now.

Publishing & Scheduling Posts in Gutenberg

The Status & Visibility options allow us to publish and schedule content. These options also allow you to choose the post format. These provide different post "templates" based on what the post contains:

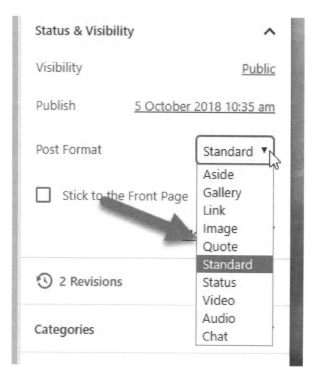

Most users will probably want to keep the default "standard" format. However, feel free to experiment and see how a post looks using these different formats. Simply publish a post using a format, view it, then come back in and change to a different format. I'll leave you to explore those, but you can read more about Post Formats on the WordPress websites if you are interested:

http://codex.WordPress.org/Post_Formats

When you have completed your post, you can save it as a draft, preview it, publish it, or schedule the post to be published at a future date.

The first two options are one-click processes:

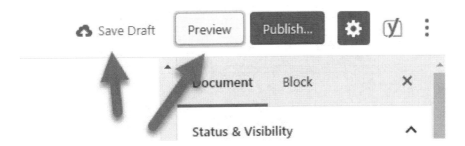

To publish or schedule your post, click the **Publish** button. You'll then see these options:

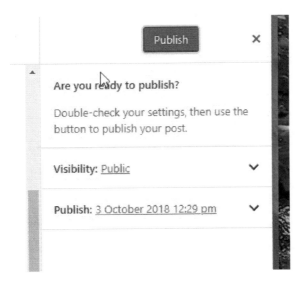

The bottom section allows you to select the date and time to publish the content. It defaults to "now", but click on the date link and it opens a calendar so you can choose to schedule the post for publication at a future time and date:

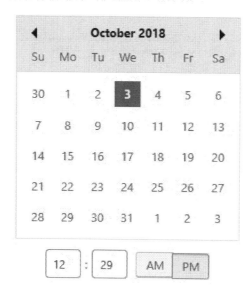

When you select a date in the future, the **Publish** button will change to **Schedule**, and upon clicking that button, the post will be scheduled to automatically publish on that date and time.

Once you've selected when to publish, click the **Publish** button at the top. The post will then be published at the selected date and time.

The **Visibility** tab of these settings defines who can see your post. Usually, you'll want it to be visible to the public, but you can choose **Private** if you only want site admins and editors to see it, or **Password Protect** if you want the post to be "locked" behind a password.

Using the HTML Editor to Edit Your Post

There may be times when you want to edit your post in raw HTML code. To do this, click on the ellipsis menu button, top right of the Gutenberg editor:

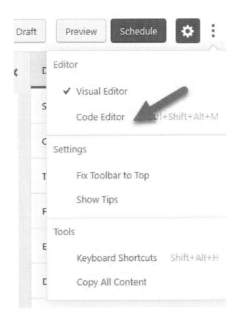

Currently, the **Visual Editor** is selected. It's what we have been using so far. If you choose **Code Editor** instead, you can view/edit the entire post as HTML code.

You can make changes in the HTML editor and save changes as required.

Yoast SEO Settings for the Post

When we installed the Yoast SEO plugin, it added a panel to the add post (and add page) screen.

If you scroll down a little, you should come across the **Yoast SEO** section.

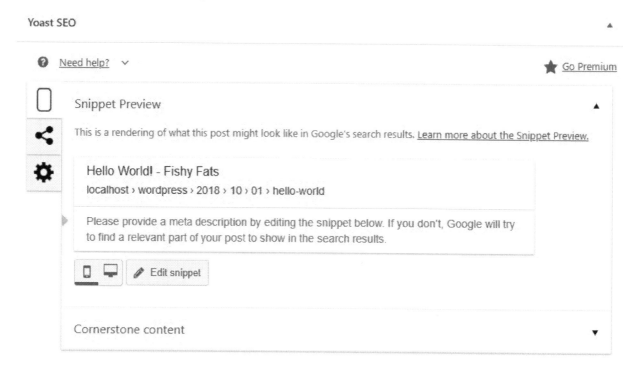

NOTE: If you don't see this section when using the Classic editor, make sure it is checked in the screen options (top right). If you are using the Gutenberg editor, there are no screen options for the edit post screen.

This Yoast SEO box looks very similar to the ones we saw for category and tag pages. The big difference is in the **Advanced** settings screen, which you access by clicking the third button down on the left (the "cog").

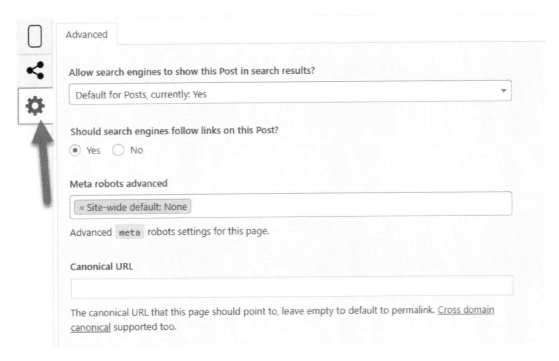

These settings give us fine control over how the search engines will deal with this post. We can use these settings to override the global settings for the site. This is powerful. With this fine level of control, we can treat every post and page on our site differently if we want to.

The top setting allows us to show/hide a post from the search engines. By default, all posts will be indexed by the search engines. If we don't want a post indexed and visible in the search engines, we can select **No** from the drop-down box (which sets the page to noindex for those that know what this means). However, this would be most unusual for posts.

The next setting is whether search engines should follow links in this post. The default is yes, but we can set them to No (which is a nofollow tag for those that know what this means). I don't recommend changing this unless you know what you are doing.

The **Meta Robots Advanced** allows us to set a few other Meta tags on our pages. Click on the edit box where it currently says **Site-wide default: None** and a drop-down box appears with options you can set:

103

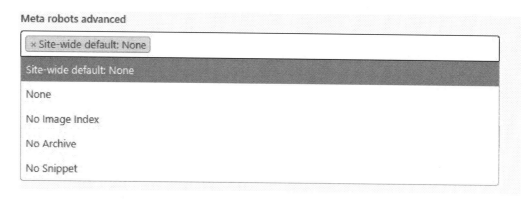

No Image Index is useful if you don't want the search engines to index the images on your page. Indexed images can be easily found within the image search on Google, and pirated.

No Archive tag tells Google not to store a cached copy of your page

No Snippet tells Google not to show a description under your Google listing (nor will it show a cached link in the search results).

The only options you may want to add occasionally is the **No Archive** option, but only in very special circumstances. There are times when we don't want Google to keep an archive (cached version), of a page. By setting the post as **No Archive** we are preventing the search engines from keeping a backup of the page.

Why might you want to do this?

Well, maybe you have a limited offer on your site and you don't want people seeing it after the offer has finished. If the page was archived, it is technically possible for someone to go in and see the last cached page at Google, which will still show your previous offer.

Editing Posts

At some point after writing a post, you may want to go in and edit or update it. This is an easy process. Just click on **All Posts** in the **Posts** menu. It will open a screen with a list of posts on your site.

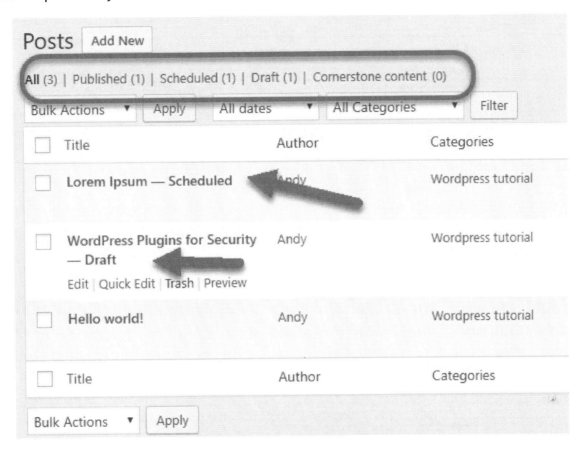

In the screenshot, you can see that I have three posts on the site. The top one is scheduled, the second one is a draft, and the third one is published.

You can view just the published, just the scheduled, or just the draft posts, by clicking on the item in the menu at the top.

What if you had a lot of posts and needed to find one?

There are two ways of doing this. One is from within your Dashboard using the available search and filtering tools. The other method is one I'll show you later and involves visiting your site while you are logged into the Dashboard.

For now, let's look at how we can find posts from within the Dashboard:

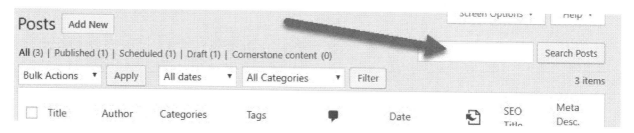

Firstly, if you know what month you wrote the post, you could show all posts from that month by selecting the month from the **All Dates** drop-down box. You can also search for a post by showing just those posts within a certain category. Select the desired category from the **All Category** drop-down box.

Perhaps the easiest way of all is to use the **Search Posts** feature. Type in a keyword phrase you know is in the title and then click the **Search Posts** button.

Once the list of matching posts is displayed, mouseover the one you want to edit and click edit from the popup menu. An even easier way is to just click the title of the post. This takes you back to the same editor screen you used when first creating the post. Make your changes in there and just click the **Update** button to save your modifications.

Revisions - Classic Editor

Whenever you make changes to a post, WordPress keeps a record (archive), of those changes. If you're using the Classis Editor, you'll find a section called **Revisions** on the edit post screen. You won't see this section if you haven't made changes to the post.

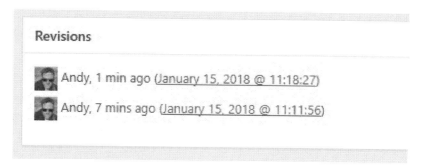

If you don't see it, make sure it is checked in the screen options from the top.

The revisions list shows all the changes that have been made to a post, including the time stamp and the user that made the edits.

You can view any previous version of the post by clicking the date link. You won't lose the current version; it just opens a viewing screen so you can see what that previous version looked like. If I click on the last revision at the top of the list (i.e. the one before the currently saved version), I see this:

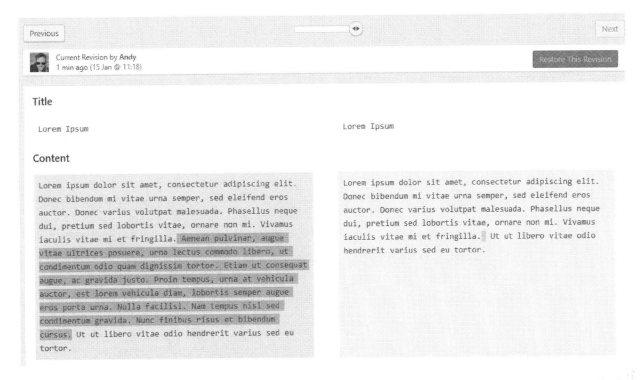

There is a link in the top left of the screen to take you back to the post editor. Click this link if you want to cancel and return to the editor.

Below this, you can see two different versions of the post. There is one on the left and one on the right. These are in chronological order, with the oldest on the left, newest on the right. The previous revision is therefore on the left, the current saved post on the right.

The differences between the two versions will be highlighted in yellow on the right (and red on the left).

At the top of the screen, you will also see a slider.

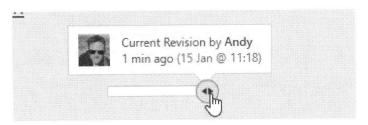

Move the slider left or right to scroll through the revisions.

Revisions – Gutenberg Editor

If you are using the Gutenberg editor, things are slightly different. You'll find the revisions section in the right panel of the editor:

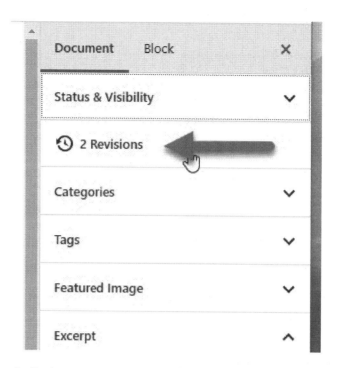

You don't get a list of all the revisions as we did with the Classic editor. Instead, you simply click the "Revisions" link to take you to the revisions screen:

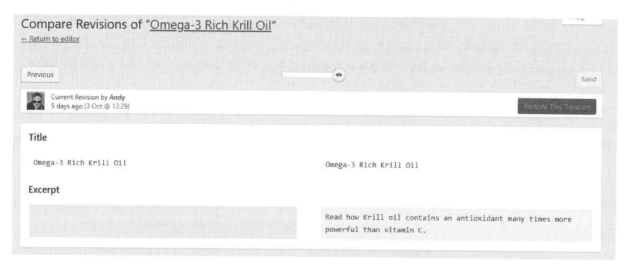

This then works the same way as it did for the Classic editor, using the slider at the top to navigate between revisions.

Why Use Revisions?

Suppose you are working on a post and delete a paragraph or change an image. Later, you ask yourself "why did I delete that?". With revisions, you can revert to previous versions of your post with a few mouse clicks.

Restoring a Revision

If you find a revision you want to restore, it's as simple as clicking the **Restore This Revision** button.

This will copy the post into the editor as it was when the revision was saved, but also create a new revision of the post you are over-writing (that means you won't lose anything). When the revision is restored, you are back on the **Post Edit** screen, but nothing is saved until you click the **Update** button.

Creating Pages – About, contact & terms

The first web pages we are going to create on the site are the ones I call "legal" pages. Remember? We talked about them earlier. These are the web pages that are not specifically written to engage our visitors but are required to make the site complete, and more professional.

Contact Form

Let's start with the Contact page. This will allow your visitors to contact you by filling out a form on your site. For this, we are going to use a plugin.

Click **Add New** in the Plugins sidebar menu.

In the search box, type **contact form 7**

You should see this plugin:

Contact Form 7

Just another contact form plugin. Simple but flexible.

By Takayuki Miyoshi

Install Now

More Details

★★★★½ (1,391)   Last Updated: 1 week ago

1+ Million Active Installations   ✔ Compatible with your version of WordPress

Click the **Install Now** button. The plugin will install, and the button will change to **Activate**. Click to **Activate** the plugin.

You will now have a new menu in the sidebar, labeled **Contact**.

Under the Contact menu, click **Contact Forms**.

The plugin installed a demo form for you, and that serves our purpose.

Highlight the **shortcode** for the form and copy it.

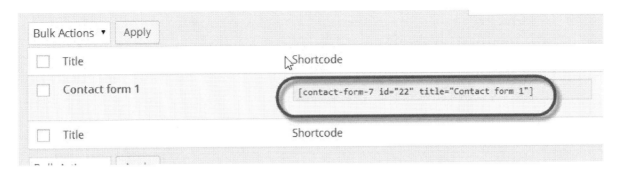

We now need to create a Page that can host the contact form. Under the **Pages** menu, click **Add New**.

For the title, type **Contact** or **Contact Us**.

In the WYSIWYG editor, paste the contact form shortcode.

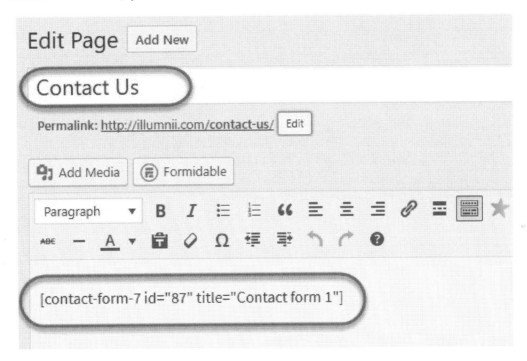

Click the **Publish** button to publish the page.

With the page published, click on the **Permalink** to the page:

The new contact page will open. Note that this is an easy way to visit any post or page on your site, directly from the editor, after it is published.

You will see your contact form on the page. If you fill it in and send a test message, you should receive it at the email address you entered as your admin email when you set WordPress up.

If you are using the Gutenberg editor the process is similar. Add a title and then paste the shortcode into the main "write your story" area here:

You'll see something like this:

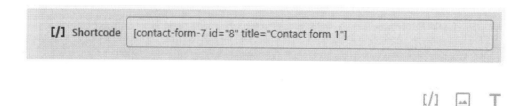

Click the **Publish** button (twice) to publish the page.

You can then click the **View Page** link to visit the page.

In WordPress, Pages don't typically have a comment section like posts. However, you can enable/disable them.

To turn comments off for the contact form (or any page where they are enabled), open the page edit screen for the contact page.

In the Classic editor, open the **Screen Options** top right, make sure **Discussion** is checked:

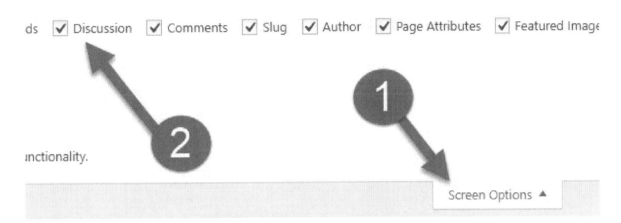

This will make the discussion section visible on the Edit Page screen:

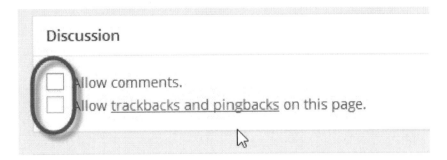

Uncheck both boxes to prevent comments and trackbacks/pingbacks.

You can now re-publish your page.

If you have already published the page, the "Publish" button is now labeled **Update**.

Once updated, go back to your contact page and you should find the comment form has gone.

That's the first page complete.

If you are using the Gutenberg editor, things are slightly different. Open the edit page screen, then on the right, you can see the **Discussion** area. Simply check or uncheck the **Allow Comments** box to turn comments for this page (or post), on or off.

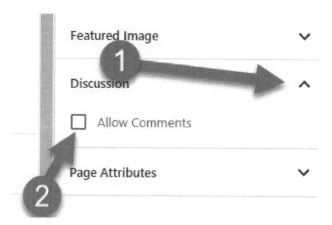

About Us Page

OK, now for the "About Us" page. This is where you have a chance to write a little bit about yourself and your site, so your visitors know about the person/company behind the site. The "About Us" page is often the most visited page on many websites, so bear that in mind.

Click **Add New** from the **Pages** sidebar menu.

This will start a new page.

For the title, use something simple, like "About", "About Me" or "About Us".

In the WYSIWYG editor, write the contents of your "About" page.

What should you include?

That is your choice, but here are some things I try to include in mine:

1. I like to begin by stating the goal of my website, but usually approach this from the point of view of the visitors. What are their problems or interests and how can my site help them.
2. Add your name and photo.
3. Add a bit of information about yourself.
4. Break up the page with bullet points and sub-headings to make it easier to read or scan.
5. Include your contact details or a link to your contact form. Note you can paste the contact form shortcode at the bottom of your about page to include it there as well if you want.

Once you have entered the text for your About page, click the **Publish** button to make it live on your site.

Visit your own about page.

You may find the comment form at the bottom of the page, so go in and turn it off if you need to.

Privacy Policy

Click on the **Privacy** link in the **Settings** menu.

The Privacy settings were introduced to help website owners get ready for GDPR compliance. If you don't know what that is, I recommend you research it a little. It is essentially a privacy law. One of the first steps in becoming compliant is to have a good privacy policy that visitors can read. This will tell them what information if any, your site collects and stores.

The Privacy options allow you to select an existing privacy policy if you already have one, or create a new one. When you create a privacy policy by clicking on the **Create New Page** button, WordPress will create a draft policy for you that you can then edit and update.

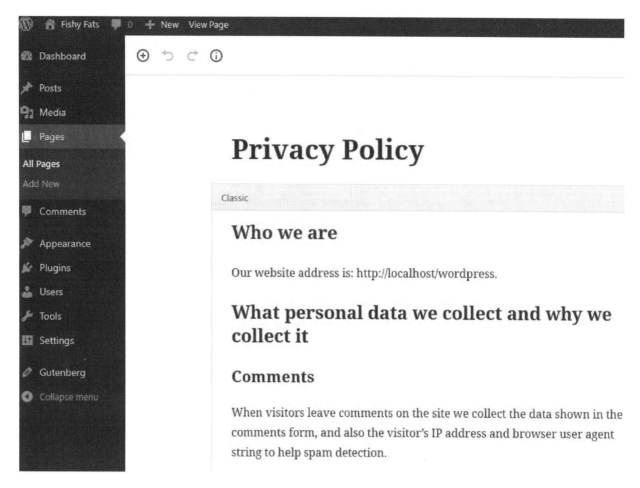

WordPress will include essential information relating to WordPress itself, but you will need to go through the policy and flesh it out. Once it is complete, save the policy. On the Privacy settings page, make sure your new privacy policy is selected:

This will ensure a link to your privacy policy is placed on the Dashboard login screen:

Terms & Disclaimer

The final pages we want to create are as follows:

1. Terms of Use
2. Possibly a Disclaimer depending on the type of stuff you have on your site.

While you can create these pages manually and add your own legal documents, I prefer to get them up quickly using another plugin.

Ideally, you would want a lawyer to draw these up for you because no plugin is going to be 100% complete, or take your personal needs into account. There are also web services out there where you can buy packs of legal documents you can update and use.

So, with that said, be aware that while I will show you a plugin to add these to your site, it is only to get you up and running quickly. I'd still recommend you get proper legal documents drawn up.

There are a few plugins out there that can create quick legal pages. The one I suggest you look at is called WP-Insert.

Wp-Insert

The Ultimate Adsense / Ad-Management Plugin for Wordpress

By Namith Jawahar

Install Now

More Details

★★★★⯪ (127)   **Last Updated:** 4 months ago

30,000+ Active Installations   ✓ **Compatible** with your version of WordPress

Install and activate it.

You'll find a new menu in the sidebar navigation labeled **Wp Insert**. Click on it to open up the settings.

Now, this plugin does a lot more than just generate legal pages. It's also a full-blown ad manager, which is useful if you want to put adverts or AdSense in your site.

For legal pages, we need to scroll down to the "Legal Pages" section:

Legal Pages

Legal Page Templates to kick start your Legal Notices.

Privacy Policy

Terms and Conditions

Disclaimer

Copyright Notice

You can see that this plugin can create a Privacy Policy (which you should have created earlier, so probably don't need), Terms and Conditions, Disclaimer and Copyright

Notice. You create all of these pages in the same way, so I'll just go through one with you.

Click on the **Terms and Conditions** link.

A dialogue box pops up, with information you need to read.

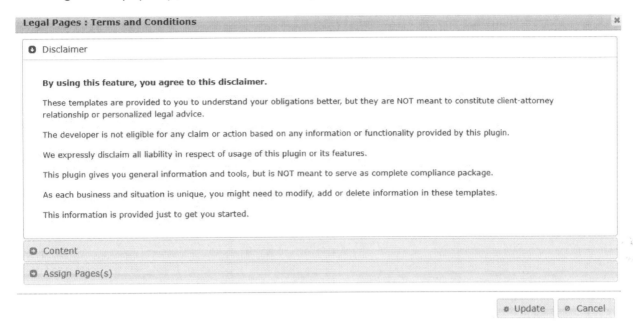

Notice that the plugin recommends you get proper legal advice for this type of document. That echoes the advice I gave you earlier.

Also, note the three tabs on the left. Disclaimer, Content and Assign Page(s).

Click on the **Content** tab. You will see the default content of the Terms and Conditions page. You can edit this if you want.

Now click on the **Assign Page(s)** tab.

Click the **Click to Generate** button.

The plugin will create a page for the document. Once done, you can see it selected in the **Assign to Page** box:

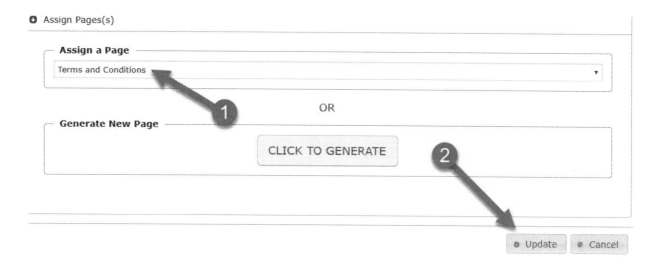

To add the content to that page, click the **Update** button.

If you click on the **Pages** link in the sidebar navigation to view all of your pages, you will now find the Terms and Conditions page.

Click on the **View** link to open the page in your web browser.

Repeat for other legal documents you want to create.

Top Navigation Menu

To make it easy for site visitors to find the legal pages, we need to create a custom menu. Let's do that now.

Under the **Appearance** menu in the left sidebar, select **Menus**. At the top, click the link to create a new menu:

You will now be able to enter a name for your menu:

I call this menu my "legal menu". Always give menus a descriptive name so you know what they are, simply by looking at the title.

Next, click the **Create Menu** button. This creates an empty menu that we can add items to. On the left, you'll see a list of your pages:

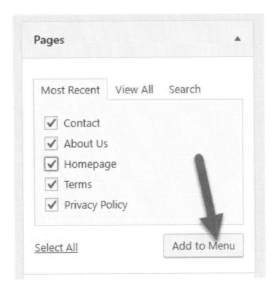

Place a checkmark next to the pages you want to be included in your menu. I've checked:

- Contact
- About Us
- Homepage
- Privacy Policy
- Terms of Use

This menu will link to all the important pages.

Once checked, click the **Add to Menu** button.

You will now see your list of pages in a column on the right. You can click and drag these pages so that they are in the order you want them to appear on your site.

You can also nest menu items, like this:

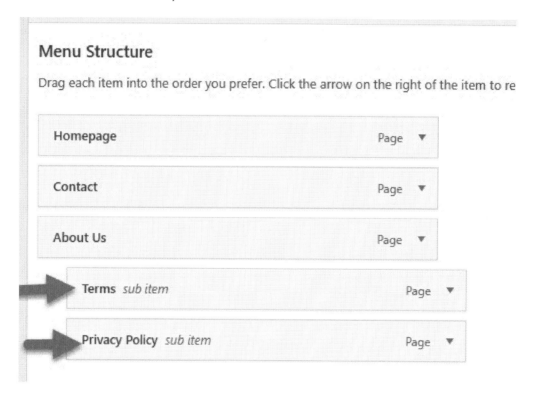

See how the Privacy Policy and the Terms of Use are indented under the "parent" About Us page?

When you indent pages in a menu, only the parent pages show in the menu on your site, but when a visitor moves their mouse over the parent page, a drop-down menu appears showing the indented pages.

Here it this menu on my site.

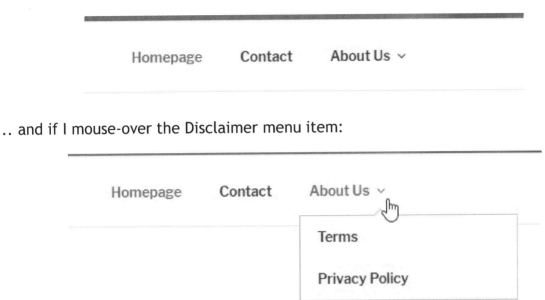

.. and if I mouse-over the Disclaimer menu item:

The exact look of this will depend on the theme you are using.

In my case, I don't want the privacy and terms nested under the About Us page, so I'll remove the indent from my menu. However, this type of nesting of menu items is useful to stop your menu from becoming too big.

To display your menu on your website, you need to tell your "theme", where to put it.

At the top of the **Menus** screen, click on the **Manage Locations** tab.

When designers are creating WordPress themes, they design them with menu locations in mind. Most themes will allow a menu at the top of the page, usually under the main site logo, but some themes will have multiple locations designed for menus.

In the Twenty Seventeen theme, there are two possible locations where you can put your menu.

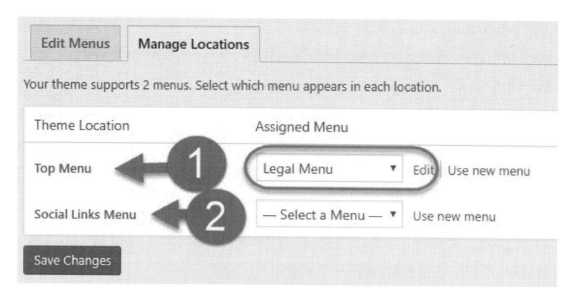

The first location is at the top of the page (the second is designed for social media links), so I've chosen my new legal menu to display there.

Save changes when done.

If you now visit your website, your menu will be visible in the location you chose.

Try clicking items in your menu. You should be taken to the corresponding pages on your site.

If you want, you can try adding the menu to other available locations (only the **social links** location in this theme), just to see where it ends up.

When you have finished playing with your menus and locations, make sure your legal menu is only displayed ONCE on your site.

Since different themes offer different options for menu locations, if you decide to change to a different WordPress theme later, you may have to re-arrange your menu(s).

While menu locations allow easy insertion of menus, you can also add menus to other locations using widgets. For example, I often add a menu into the sidebar of a site, and that requires a widget. We'll look at widgets later.

Creating the Categories

OK, so the site is starting to take shape, but we need to start adding the content that we WANT our visitors reading. This is where we start adding posts. Before we do that, we need to set up some categories which will be the filing system for these posts.

Setting up the Categories

I always like to start by creating the first few categories for the posts I know I want to write. You can create categories on the fly, as you need them. However, since I have already planned my site, I know three categories I will be using. Remember this:

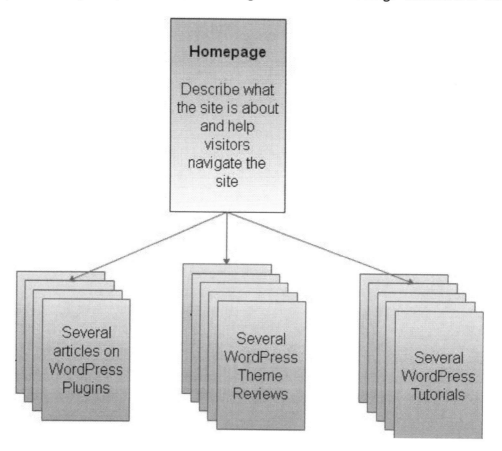

So, I have categories for:

1. Plugins
2. Themes
3. Tutorials

Let's set up those categories now. They won't appear on the site until a post is added to the category, so you don't end up with empty categories.

Click **Categories** under the **Posts** menu in the left sidebar.

On the right of the categories screen, you can see a list of all existing categories. The only one you have now is **Uncategorized**. This is the one that WordPress set up to be used as a default category. If you enter a post and forget to select a category, WordPress would choose this one by default.

I want my "tutorials" category to be the default category. The easiest way to do this is to edit the "Uncategorized" category.

If you move your mouse over "Uncategorized", a menu appears:

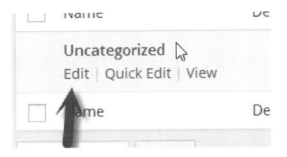

Click **Edit**.

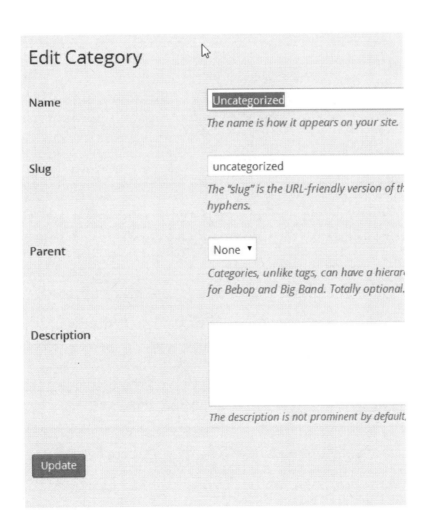

You can now edit this category.

Enter the name of your chosen default category. In my case, it's "tutorials".

Delete the contents of the **Slug** box, and leave it empty. The slug is the text that will be used in the URL of posts in this category. If the slug is blank when you save your category, WordPress will use the category name to create a slug, with spaces being replaced by dashes.

Leave the **Parent** box as **None**. Choosing a parent allows you to nest categories in much the same way we did with menu items when constructing the legal menu. I don't want nested categories, so no "Parent".

In the description box, enter a few sentences to describe the purpose of the category.

When you have finished, click the **Update** button.

If you go back and look at your categories, your new default category will be listed in place of the old "Uncategorized" category:

Note that third column "Slug". WordPress has given my "tutorials" category the slug "tutorials". That is, the same as the category name. This will now create URLs that look like this:

http://mysite.com/tutorials/using-an-image-for-the-logo

Note that you can enter a slug when creating your categories. This can be useful if you want the slug to be different from the category name.

To enter new categories, just add the information on the left side of the **Categories** page and click the **Add New Category** button when done:

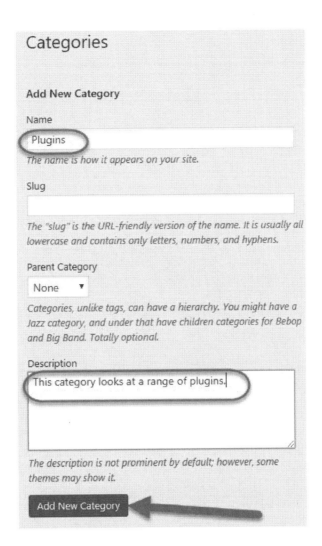

Here is my final list of three categories.

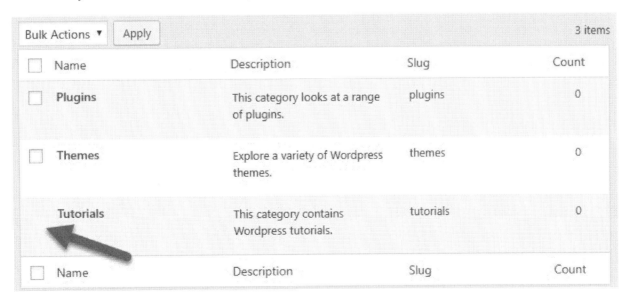

I'll add more as and when I need them.

You'll notice that the default category is the one without a checkbox next to it. Since this category cannot be deleted, the checkbox is missing.

OK, I've got the categories to set up. Let's enter the first post.

Creating Posts Workflow

Create a new, blank post. To do this, select **Add New** from the **Posts** menu in the left sidebar.

You now have a blank post, ready for entry. It doesn't matter whether you choose to use the Gutenberg editor of the Classic editor. However, if you do use the Classic editor, make sure you enable **Excerpt** in the screen options.

OK, we are now ready to enter a post.

Enter a title

Make sure the title tells the visitor what the post is about, without being overly long. For my first post, I'll call it:

"Recommended Web Hosts and Registrars"

This will be a post about recommended web hosting companies and registrars.

Typing in the post content

You can type your content directly into the WYSIWYG/Gutenberg editor, and that is what I do. However, some people prefer to write their content in Microsoft Word first and then copy it across to WordPress. If you are using the Classic editor, there is a downside. Word tends to add in some formatting code that you really do not want.

```
<h3><a name="_Toc529277431"></a>Typing in the post content</h3>
You can type your      ent directly into the WYSIWYG/Gutenberg editor, and that
some people prefer       rite their content in Microsoft Word first and then co
WordPress.  The downsid     is that you cannot retain formatting from Word, so yo
paste as plain text.  That eans reformatting everything once the text is in

In the Classic editor, you can paste a Word document as follows:
<ol>
        <li>Select all the text in Word, and copy it.</li>
        <li>In WordPress, click the <strong>Paste as Text</strong> button in
will strip out extra code fr   the Word content.</li>
        <li>Paste into Wor    ress, and reformat.</li>
</ol>
If you are using the G   enberg editor,
<h3><a name="_Toc529277432"></a>Select a category</h3>
Once the post is complete,  choose a category.  I have three to choose from (th
```

It is, therefore, a better idea to paste as text only, and reformat in the WordPress dashboard. This is not an issue with the Gutenberg editor, as that seems to paste in cleanly.

To copy a Word document to your post using the Classic editor:

1. Select all the text in Word, and copy it.

2. In WordPress, click the **Paste as Text** button in the editor toolbar. This will strip out extra code from the Word content.

3. Paste into WordPress, and reformat.

If you are using the Gutenberg editor, simply copy the Word document and paste it into the main "story" window. You should find your formatting is largely preserved.

Select a category

Once the post is complete, choose a category. I have three to choose from (though I could create another one if needed).

You select the category by checking the appropriate box in the **Categories** section of the **Edit Post** screen:

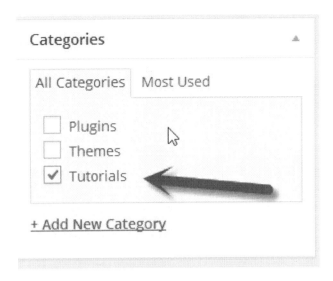

Note that there is an **Add New Category** link underneath the existing categories. This allows you to quickly add other categories when you need them. However, adding a category via this link will not give you the option of adding a category description, so I personally add categories the way I showed you earlier.

Do you need tags?

Since this is my first post, I won't be adding any tags. As I add more posts to the site, I will consider whether they are needed. It is easy enough to go back in and add them to posts, so you don't have to do everything at the time of publishing.

Add an Excerpt

We talked about excerpts earlier in the book. I recommend you add an excerpt for all posts on your site.

Enter a two or three sentence summary of the post. Your visitors will probably read this excerpt as a description of the post on certain pages of your site. Therefore, try to get in their heads and figure out what would make them click through to read the post? Enter that as the excerpt.

Post Formats

Some WordPress themes provide you with a number of "templates" to style each post you create. The Twenty Seventeen theme has several. You'll find them listed in the post **Format** section of the **Edit Post** screen:

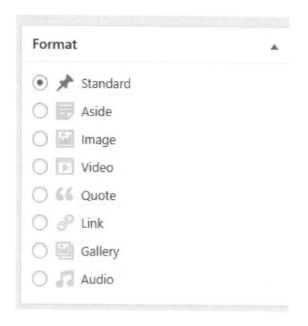

The default format is "Standard" and this is what you should use for most posts on your site. If you select one of the other formats, the layout of that post will change. Each format is designed for a specific purpose, some of which are self-explanatory because of the name of the format. However, since all themes are different, the formats you see above will not be the same in all themes. By all means, try the different formats and visit your post to see the layout of that format.

After exploring these formats, don't forget to go back and change it to "Standard" if that is what you want. Always remember to "Update" your posts after any editing.

OK, everything is entered. Click the **Publish** button to make your post live on your site.

What to do next?

You can now go off and start writing posts on your website. However, as you do, keep an eye on what is happening with your website. For example, the latest posts are displayed on my homepage, with the last published post at the top. I prefer to have a more "static" homepage, without displaying my latest posts like that, so I'll show you how to do that soon.

Have a look at your website.

Is there a sidebar on the homepage?

Is there anything inside the sidebar?

I have several items in my sidebar. These have been added to the sidebar using widgets:

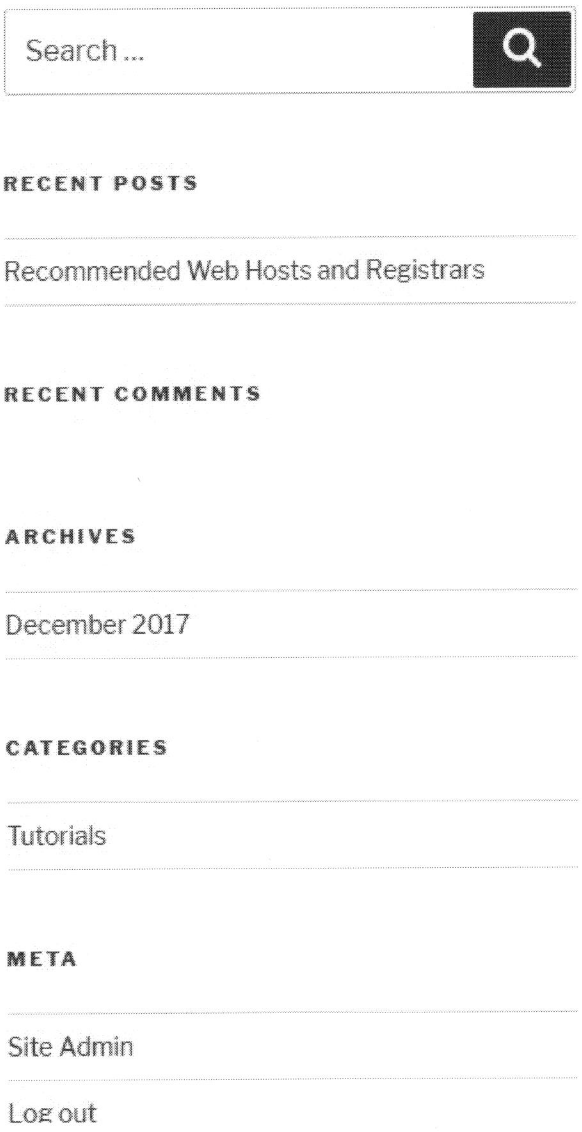

Search ... 🔍

RECENT POSTS

Recommended Web Hosts and Registrars

RECENT COMMENTS

ARCHIVES

December 2017

CATEGORIES

Tutorials

META

Site Admin

Log out

In the screenshot above, you can see a widget at the top to add search functionality to the site. Under this are widgets that add **Recent Posts, Recent Comments, Archives, Categories** and finally one called **Meta** which helps login, logout, access RSS feeds, etc.

You have total control over which widgets you want to use in the sidebar. Some themes even allow you to add widgets to other areas of the web page, like the footer.

Let's look at widgets in more detail.

Widgets

From the **Appearance** menu in the left sidebar, select **Widgets.**

Think of widgets as features you can add to your website. We mentioned a few widgets towards the end of the previous section (recent posts, archives, categories etc).

In the Widgets section of the Dashboard, you can see a list of all available widgets, as well as the places you can put them on your website.

The Twenty Seventeen theme gives you three places on your site where you can insert widgets:

1. Blog Sidebar
2. Footer 1
3. Footer 2

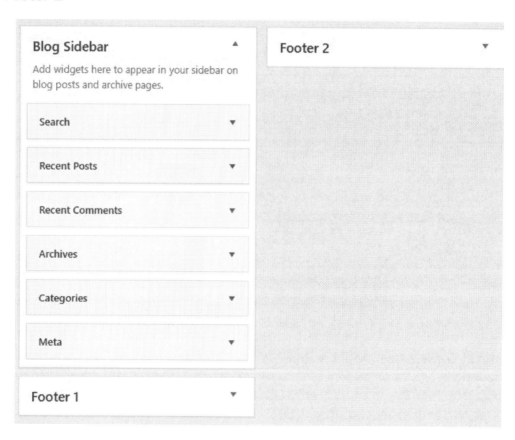

You can see the widgets on the blog sidebar. These are the widgets that added those features to the sidebar in the last section of the book.

Each widget will have some options you can change. These can be accessed by clicking the down arrow on the right of the widget.

For example, here are the options for the Search box:

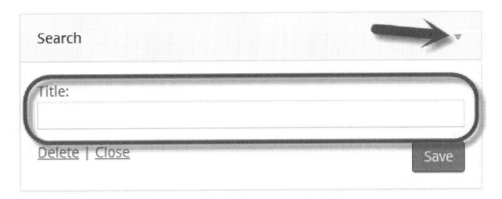

OK, so the only option is to give it a title. At the moment, there isn't a title, and this is how it looks on my site:

Since the search box has the word "Search" inside, there really isn't a need to give this widget a title. However, feel free to experiment with your own site widgets.

Notice that in the widget options, you also have a delete option if you don't want to use that widget.

The Recent Posts widget has a couple of options:

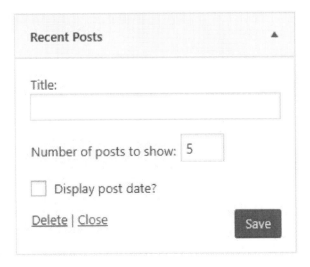

Again, there is no title specified, yet if we look at the site, we see this:

RECENT POSTS

Recommended Web Hosts and Registrars

What? There is a title...

If you leave the title blank for a widget, WordPress will use the default title for that widget, in this case, "Recent Posts". In the case of the Search widget, there was no default title.

If you want to change that title to something else, you can enter a title into your widget options:

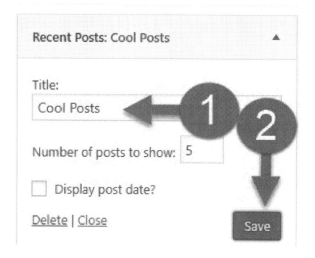

Here is what this looks like on my site:

COOL POSTS

Recommended Web Hosts and Registrars

This widget also lets you choose how many recent posts to display and you can even get the widget to display the dates of each post if you want.

I will leave you to explore the other sidebar widgets that were installed by default.

Open the options and look at how you can configure each widget. Feel free to change settings and see how they affect the display of the widget on the site.

For my site, I don't want recent comments, archives or the Meta widget. Deleting a widget is easy. Open the options for the widget, then click the Delete link.

Note that you can also re-order widgets in the sidebar by dragging and dropping in the Widget screen of the Dashboard. I want to move the Category widget so that it appears right below the search box:

My sidebar looks a lot cleaner:

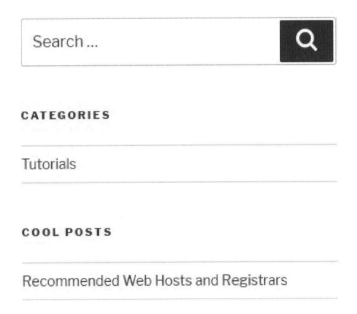

Other widget areas

OK, so we've covered the blog sidebar. However, the Twenty Seventeen theme also allows us to place widgets in the Footer 1 and Footer 2 areas.

Different themes will allow widgets in different areas, so there is little point in going over these widget areas in any detail. The best thing you can do is to put a widget into a widgetized area and see where it appears on your site.

It should come as no surprise if I tell you the two "footer areas" are at the bottom of the web page.

Something to try: Add a Custom Menu widget to a footer area. In the settings of the widget, choose your legal menu. Save, and check out your site.

It is wise to remember that when you add widgets to one of these areas, it will appear on all posts/pages on your site that include that widgetized area. For example, some themes don't include a sidebar on the homepage, but the sidebar is included on all posts. Therefore, a widget placed in the sidebar won't appear on the homepage but would appear on all posts.

There are ways to only include certain widgets in specific categories, posts or pages, but you'll need a WordPress plugin to achieve that. We'll look at one later in this book.

Other available widgets

WordPress installs a basic stock of widgets for you to use and you can experiment with those to see what they do. Some plugins you install will also add new widgets to your dashboard. For example, I often use a plugin called **Formidable Forms**, and when that is installed, it adds a couple of widgets that help insert forms into my web pages:

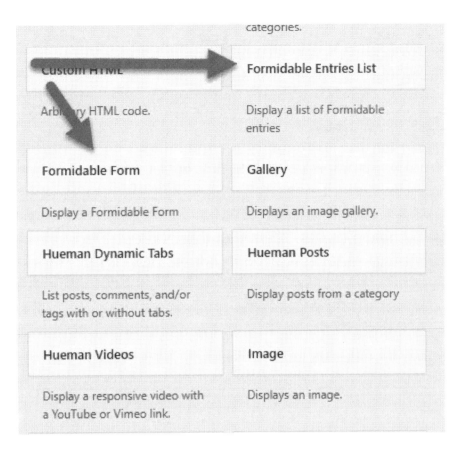

The "Hueman" widgets in that screenshot were added by a WordPress theme, called the Hueman theme.

Have fun experimenting with the widgets, and your theme. We are going to move on and consider a very special page.

The Homepage.

The Homepage - A special case

By default, WordPress will show your recent posts on the homepage. I personally don't like this and prefer total control over what is displayed on my homepage. In fact, I create a page of content to use for my homepage and show that instead of a list of posts. This is easy in WordPress. We simply set up the homepage to show a "static" page.

The first step in achieving this is to create a new WordPress page to use as our Homepage.

Go and click on the **Add New** item in the **Pages** sidebar menu.

Give your page a title that will be displayed at the top of your homepage.

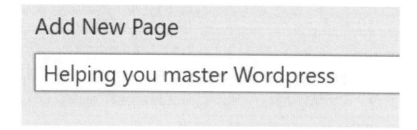

Add the content you want to be displayed on your homepage using the WYSIWYG editor.

After clicking the **Publish** button to make it live, your homepage will still look the same. It still lists the most recent posts...

Don't panic. That's simply because we have not told WordPress to use the new page as a homepage.

To do that, go to the **Reading** settings inside the **Settings** menu in the left sidebar.

Select **A static page** from the **Your homepage displays** section and then choose your newly created page from the **Homepage** drop down box.

Click the **Save Changes** button to finish.

If you now visit the homepage of your site, you'll no longer see your most recent posts in the main area of the homepage. Instead, you will find the WordPress page you just created.

If you see a comment box at the bottom of the homepage, you know how to turn it off. If you don't see a comment form and want one, you know how to turn it on. Personally, I don't include a comment form on my homepage.

You might not like the overall look and feel of your site at the moment. However, later in the book, I'll show you how to change that, any time you like. It only takes seconds and you can choose from an almost unlimited variety of styles.

For now, you should concentrate on adding content to the site. For each category you added, you should add some posts.

While you are working on that, we can consider some other important factors, starting with visitor interaction.

Allowing Comments

I love getting comments from real people wanting to engage me on the site or add their own tips, ideas, or thoughts on a post. However, comments are also a major source of frustration because spammers can flood your inbox with hundreds of automated spam comments. Because of this, a lot of webmasters turn them off. You should not turn them off because real visitors like to comment on your posts. Just as importantly, the search engines love to see a website that actively engages its visitors.

So, what is the problem with spammers and how can we stop them?

Well, if you don't already know, you soon will. Spammers see comments on other people's websites as a way to make their own web pages rank better. You see, when a comment is approved, it links back to the website that was entered into the comment form.

Leave a Reply

Your email address will not be published. Required fields are marked *

Comment

Name *

Email *

Website

Post Comment

So, approved comments are seen as links, and links that point to a site help boost it in Google!

Because of the problems with spammers, we have already set up WordPress so that all comments need to be manually approved. There are also plugins you can install to help cut down on spam comments.

Akismet Anti-Spam

WordPress will install Akismet by default. It is an excellent anti-spam plugin that is free for non-commercial sites. However, if you have a commercial site, the plugin does require you pay for a commercial license.

When you activate the plugin, you'll see a banner across the top of your dashboard:

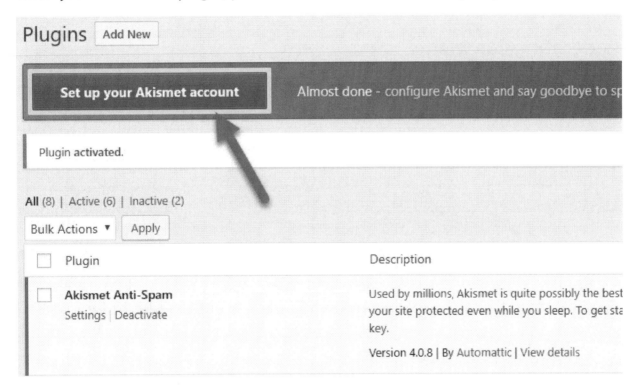

Click the setup button.

A screen opens that has a button to **Get your API key**. Click it and you'll be taken to the Akismet plugin page.

Click the button to Activate Akismet. You'll be taken to a pricing table to select your plan. Follow the instructions to get your API key.

Once you have your key, paste it into the API Key box and click on the **Connect** button.

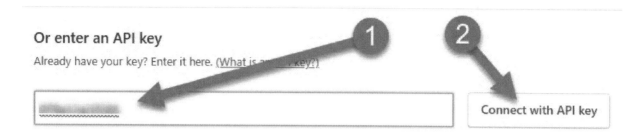

Activate Akismet

Log in or sign up now.

Get your API key

Or enter an API key

Already have your key? Enter it here. (What is a ~~API key?~~)

Connect with API key

You will see a few options, but essentially your site is now protected from spam by Akismet.

Moderating Comments

We have already seen the comments screen when we looked at the demo comment installed by WordPress, so you should already have a pretty good idea of how this all works.

When someone comes to your site and leaves a comment, it is checked against our blacklist (we set that up earlier). If the comment contains a word or phrase in the blacklist, it is sent to the spam folder. If it passes the checks and also passes the checks by the WP-SpamShield plugin, the comment is added to the "Pending" list. At this point, WordPress sends an email to your admin email address telling you there is a comment to moderate. That email is useful because it contains links to approve, trash, or spam the comment.

```
A new comment on the post "Recommended Web Hosts and Registrars" is waiting for your approval
http://rapidwpsites.com/tutorials/recommended-web-hosts-and-registrars/

Author : My Web Host (IP: 88.18.143.85 , 85.Red-88-18-143.staticIP.rima-tde.net)
E-mail : andy@mywebhost.com
URL    : http://mywebhost.com
Whois  : http://whois.arin.net/rest/ip/88.18.143.85
Comment:
Give me a link back.

Approve it: http://rapidwpsites.com/wp-admin/comment.php?action=approve&c=3
Trash it: http://rapidwpsites.com/wp-admin/comment.php?action=trash&c=3
Spam it: http://rapidwpsites.com/wp-admin/comment.php?action=spam&c=3
Currently 1 comment is waiting for approval. Please visit the moderation panel:
http://rapidwpsites.com/wp-admin/edit-comments.php?comment_status=moderated
```

You can click the relevant link in the email to moderate the comment if you like. I personally like to log into the Dashboard to moderate comments. When you log in to your Dashboard and there are comments waiting, you will see a visual indicator of comments awaiting moderation:

Clicking on the **Comments** menu item takes you to the moderation screen.

Move your mouse over a comment and a menu appears:

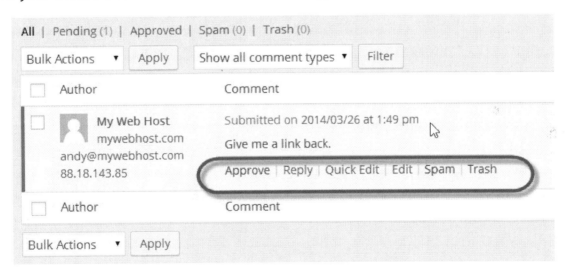

From there, you can approve the comment, or send it to spam or trash.

I highly recommend that you are very strict about approving comments. If you do not know the commenter (i.e. they are not a friend or a frequent visitor you know of), then never approve a comment that does not add to the conversation on the post they are commenting on.

For example, on my web hosting post, I would trash all of the following comments:

"Love the site, great work!"

"What theme are you using, it looks great".

"I love this site"

"Fantastic article. I will send my friend over to read it".

"I think you have a problem with browser compatibility".

Incidentally, these are all very common spam comments whose sole purpose is to get a link back to a website. Quite often, spam comments try to flatter you into approving them.

Do you see how none of these are about web hosting? These comments could have been made on ANY post. That is often the sign of a spammer at work.

I tend to only approve comments that add to the "discussion" started by the post. I'd also approve a comment that was obviously written by someone who had read the post and wanted help or advice related to the post. Comments are there for you to interact, help and discuss with your audience. Any comment that does not add to the conversation should be trashed.

When you have comments in the trash, or spam folders, you will eventually need to go in and empty the trash (or empty the spam folder). Just click on the tab (in the screenshot below I have clicked onto the **Trash** tab):

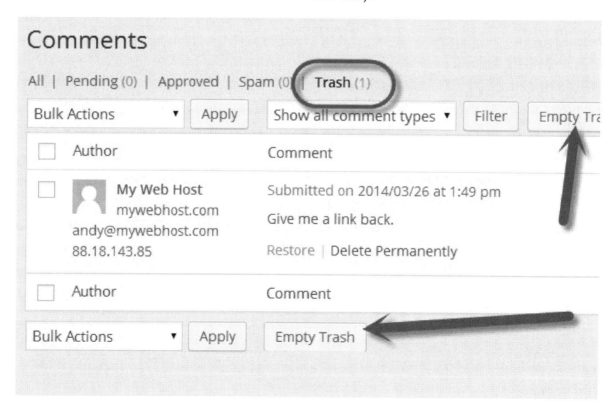

Then click the Empty Trash button.

On the spam screen, there is an "Empty Spam" button.

So, what is the difference between spam and trash?

Well, there isn't a lot of difference. WordPress and many anti-spam plugins will send suspicious comments to the spam folder as a place to hold them until you moderate them. Everything in the spam folder will be suspicious, so have a quick glance down to see if there is anything worth approving. Some anti-spam plugins will check IP and email addresses of comments in the spam folder, and send any further comments from those "spammers" directly to the spam folder.

If there is anything worth approving, you can move your mouse over the comment, and click the "Not Spam" link.

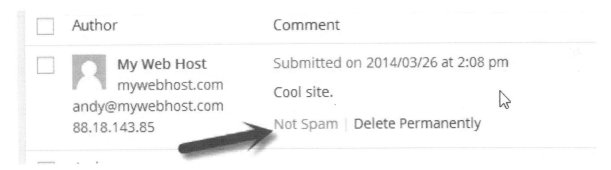

That will send it to the Pending tab.

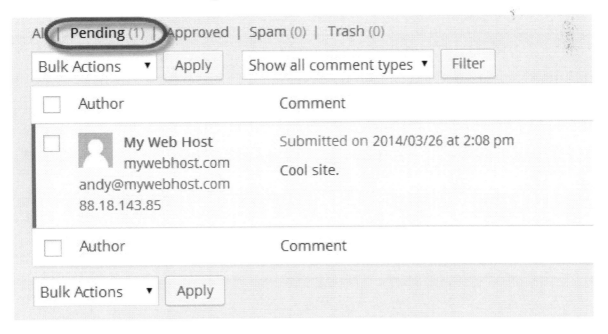

From there, you can approve the comment if you want.

Social Sharing?

You put a lot of effort into your website, so wouldn't it be nice to give your visitors an easy way for them to share your content with their friends?

Social sharing plugins make this easy.

There are a huge number of different social sharing plugins to choose from. We'll install a popular one here.

Click **Add New** from the Plugins sidebar menu.

Search for **Social Pug**.

Find, install, and activate, this one:

You'll find the plugin adds a **Social Pug** menu directly into the left sidebar.

Click on the Social Pug link.

You have a couple of options in terms of where the sharing buttons appear. You can have a floating sidebar that "floats" on the side of your web page, displaying the buttons. You can also have inline buttons that appear before or after your content. I am going to choose both, to show you what they look like.

When you activate one of the two options, the **Settings** for that option become available:

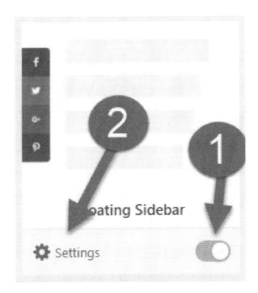

Click the settings link, and you get more options.

The first thing you need to do is select the networks you want to use:

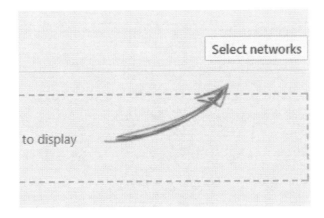

When you click the **Select Networks** button, you get to choose from the most popular sharing sites:

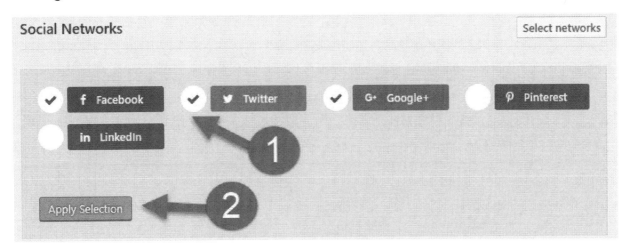

Check the sites you want to include, then click the **Apply Selection** button.

Your chosen networks will appear in a list (that you can re-order by dragging and dropping).

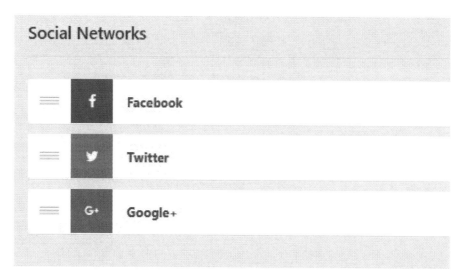

Below this list, you can choose a number of options for the style of button. I will leave you to explore those yourself. However, at the bottom, an important setting is this one:

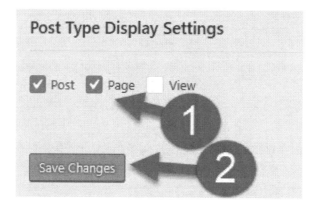

If you want the social sharing buttons on pages as well (especially if you are using a static page for the homepage), then make sure you check the **Page** type too and save changes.

If you now visit a web page on your site, you should see the social buttons "floating" as you scroll down the page:

If you have selected **Inline** buttons, click on the **Inline Content** link in the menu, and configure those in the same way. Here are some I did earlier ☺

HELPING YOU MASTER WORDPRESS

Discounts on ALL of my Udemy courses

Below you'll find a list of all of my courses. If you want to be notified of new courses, or special course promotions, p

WordPress SEO

These buttons are shown before the content of my page. Note that you can show different buttons on inline and floating panels if you want to.

Your visitors can click these buttons to share your post on Facebook, Twitter, Pinterest, Google Plus, etc. This, in turn, can bring more traffic to your site from these social networks.

Website Navigation

Someone landing on your website for the first time will have no idea what content is on your site or how to find it. It is therefore vital that you have good website navigation.

On sites I build, I make sure the following navigation is in place:

1. A homepage that tries to help the visitor find what they want. That can literally mean writing out instructions, using graphics, or just making the sidebar and menu navigation speak for itself.
2. A search box. This is already installed on the site as a widget. The default search box that comes with WordPress is poor. A better option is to add a custom Google search box which offers far more relevant search results from your site. It is beyond the scope of this book to show you how to do this, but Google it, if interested.
3. A Main menu offering contact, about and other "legal" pages. This does not always need to be in the header area of your site. I often put this type of menu in the footer widget area.
4. A recent posts widget in the sidebar of my site. Visitors can quickly see the recent articles I have written, and use those as a starting point for investigating my site.
5. Every post on my site will have a related posts section, which lists other posts that I think a visitor may be interested in.

The only one on that list we have not seen so far is the related posts plugin. Let's install and configure that now.

Related Posts With YARPP

This plugin allows you to set up a "Related Articles" section at the end of your posts. This will automatically create links to related articles on your site.

Go to the **Add New** Plugin screen and search for **yarpp**.

Yet Another Related Posts Plugin (YARPP)

Install Now

More Details

Display a list of related posts on your site based on a powerful unique algorithm.

By Adknowledge

★★★★☆ (169)

200,000+ Active Installations

Last Updated: 2 years ago

Untested with your version of WordPress

Install and activate the plugin.

You will now find the YARPP settings in the main settings menu:

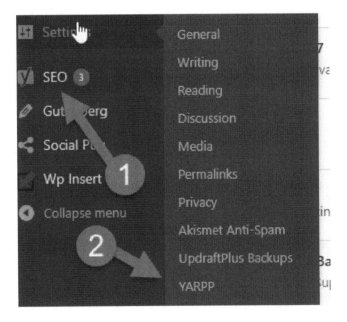

Click on **YARPP** so we can set this up.

At the top of the YARPP settings, is "The Pool". The pool is the set of posts that can be used for building a related articles section. If you decide you don't want any posts in a particular category showing up in the related articles sections on your site, you can exclude that category here by checking the box next to that category.

I am going to leave the pool defaults as they are.

If you think you won't be changing these settings, you can hide "The Pool" by unchecking the option in the **Screen Options.**

The next settings on the page are the "Relatedness" options. This defines how closely related an article needs to be, to be shown as a "related post".

I recommend you leave the relatedness options with their default values. The only change I make on smaller sites is to change the Match Threshold to a 1. On larger sites, a 2 is OK.

Next up are the **Display options for your website.**

There is plenty of scope for playing around here as well, including using your own template, but we are going to again use the default settings, with one exception. Place a checkmark next to **Show Excerpt?** This will give our related posts a description, which is taken from the excerpt we write. When you check that box, a few more options appear. Change Excerpt length to 50 (I recommend that you experiment with this setting).

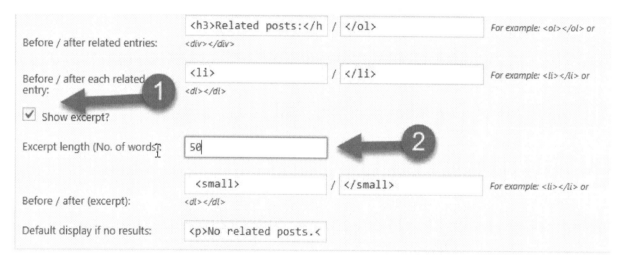

Ok, that is all we are changing. Scroll to the bottom and click **Save Changes.**

You will now have a related posts section at the end of every post on the site. You probably won't see much yet because you don't have content on the site. Here is what I see at the end of my post on this demo site:

Sharing is caring!

Welcome to WordPress. This is your first post. Edit or delete it, then start writing!

No related posts.

However, as you start adding content, the related posts section will start to populate with recommendations for your visitors.

Here is an example of a related posts section on one of my sites using this plugin.

Related Posts:

1. January 2016 Google Algorithm Updates
   January 2016 saw some major updates in Google, with wild swings in the rankings of many sites. What do we know about this update?...

2. Google Penguin, and other Google News
   Google's Penguin 4.0 is coming soon. What can you expect and how can you get ready for it?...

3. Finding Hot Niches
   If you have ever had problems identifying niches, or you have built a site that you thought would be profitable, and its wasn't, then Gary Harvey might have the answer with his latest offering – "Finding Hot Niches". This site is dedicated to showing you the best resources for researching...

This "related posts" section was on an article about search engine optimization on my ezSEONews.com site. Can you see the benefits? People who are reading the main SEO article are shown other articles that are related to what they've just been reading about. It gives us another chance to keep the visitor on our site.

Keeping WordPress Updated & Secure

WordPress is updated frequently to:

1. Add new features.
2. Fix bugs in the older version.

While some bugs are inconvenient but harmless (e.g. a feature not quite working as it should), others cause security problems for your site. Very occasionally a bug is found that could allow hackers to get into your website, through a "back door". These types of bugs need to be fixed as soon as possible and are usually fixed within hours of being found.

Fortunately, these bugs are rare. BUT... it does mean that you should always keep WordPress updated to the latest version.

When you installed your site, you may have had the option to enable an auto-upgrade script, so upgrades will be largely automatic.

If you don't have automatic updates "switched on", don't worry. Upgrading manually is very easy.

When you log in to the Dashboard, there is an **Updates** item in the **Dashboard** menu.

This will notify when there are updates available, much like the notification we saw earlier with comments to moderate. You can then click through to the **Updates** area, and update the files.

The "Updates" area lists all available updates for WordPress itself, plugins and themes.

When a WordPress upgrade is available, you'll see something like this:

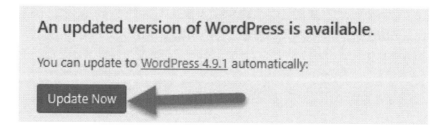

Just click the **Update Now** button and the upgrade will proceed automatically on its own. You may have to click a button or two to "upgrade the database" or some other task, but that's as technical as it gets. Just follow the instructions on the screen and you'll be fine.

If there are plugins to update, you'll see something like this:

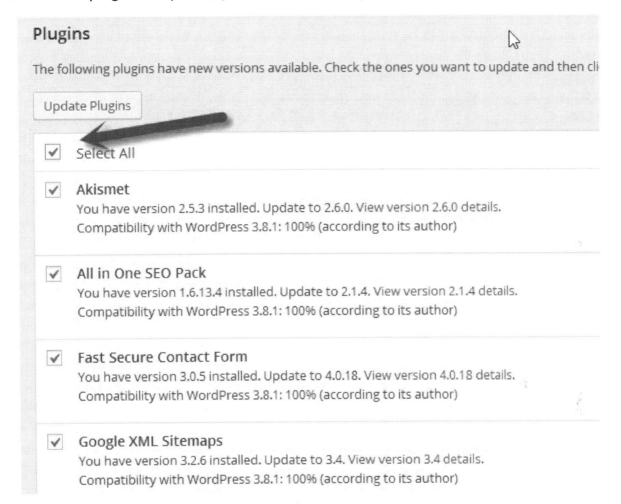

You can check one or more plugins to update, or click the **Select All** checkbox, which selects all plugins for updating. Then, simply click the **Update Plugins** button, and WordPress does the rest for you.

When your theme(s) needs updating, you'll see something like this:

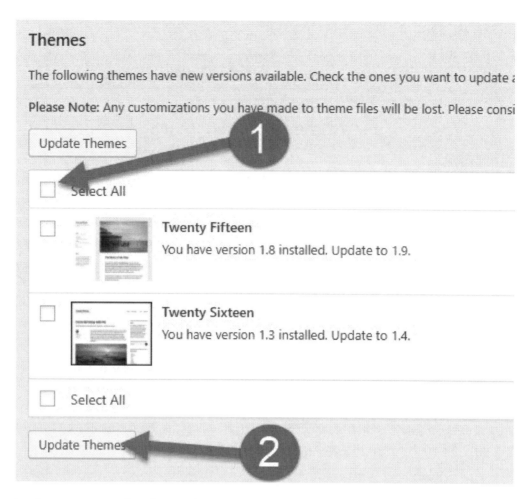

Check the box next to the theme(s) you want to update, and click the **Update Themes** button.

Backing up the Site

Backing up anything on a computer should be a priority. While good web hosts do keep backups for you, if your site gets infected with any kind of malicious code, and you don't find out about it for a while, all of your backups can be infected, and therefore not much use.

I always recommend you have some kind of backup plan, and fortunately, there is a great plugin that can help.

UpdraftPlus

Click the **Add New** item in the **Plugins** menu.

Search for Updraft.

Find, install, and activate, this plugin:

UpdraftPlus WordPress Backup Plugin

Backup and restoration made easy. Complete backups; manual or scheduled (backup to Dropbox, S3, Google Drive, Rackspace, FTP, SFTP, email + others).

By UpdraftPlus.Com, DavidAnderson

Install Now

More Details

★★★★★ (2,808)

1+ Million Active Installations

Last Updated: 2 weeks ago

✓ **Compatible** with your version of WordPress

You'll have a new **UpdraftPlus Backups** section in the settings menu. Click on it to access the settings of this plugin.

You can take manual backups on the **Backup/Restore** tab:

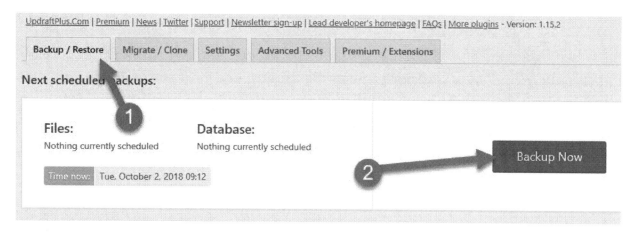

More powerful still is the ability to schedule automatic backups of your site. To do that, click on the **Settings** tab.

Choose a frequency and the number of backups to retain.

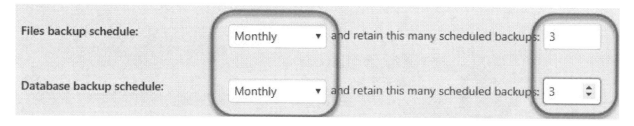

Now scroll down and click **Save Changes** at the bottom.

You will notice that on this screen, you also have the option of using remote storage for your backups. If you have a Dropbox account, that is a great place to send backups. They'll be off your server, and safe if you ever need them. You can also get backups emailed to you, though full backups can be very large.

I won't go into details on setting this up, just follow the instructions that are included with the plugin.

Changing the Look & Feel of the site

By now you should have a fully functioning website and know how to add more content to the site. However, you might not like the look of your site. Maybe the colors, the fonts, or the layout, don't look right to you. That is where themes come in.

WordPress was created to be modular in nature so that developers could create add-ons. We've seen some of these in the form of plugins and widgets, but another major way you can customize your site is by changing the WordPress theme.

Think of themes as skins. You can add a skin over the top of your content, which changes the look and feel, but doesn't touch your underlying data (content, installed plugins, etc.).

The quickest way to experience themes is to look at the ones WordPress installed on your server when you installed WordPress.

Go to **Themes** in the **Appearance** menu of your Dashboard.

Here you should find Twenty Seventeen and some possibly a couple of other default WordPress themes.

You can change the theme to one of the other installed themes, quickly and easily.

When you move your mouse over a theme thumbnail, it changes to include two buttons. A **Live Preview** button allows you to see what the theme would look like IF you activated it, and an **Activate** button to change to that theme.

Go ahead and change themes, then visit your homepage to see how different it looks.

Note that when you switch between themes, you may need to move your widgets around after the switch, or even re-add them. This is because all themes are different and have different widget areas, with different names. WordPress does its best when you switch themes but often doesn't get it quite right.

With any theme you want to use, you need to check to see where you can add widgets. Another thing to check is how many menus it can accommodate, and where those menus are located.

Where to get free themes

WordPress makes it easy for you to find and install themes for your site.

Click on **Themes** in the **Appearance** menu.

At the top of the Theme page, click the **Add New** button.

You will be taken to an "Add Themes" screen.

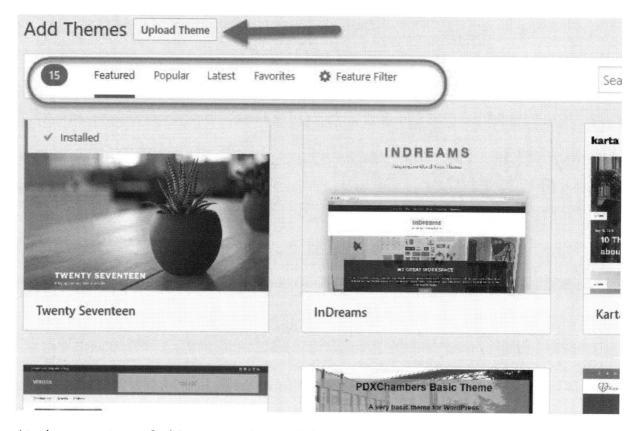

At the very top of this screen is an Upload Theme button. If you've bought or downloaded a theme from a website, it will be zipped up. Just click the Upload Theme button and upload the zipped file. The theme will install and you can then preview or activate it.

Next, on this screen, you'll see a menu across the top, with "Featured" selected. This menu gives you access to "Featured", "Popular" and "Latest" themes in the WordPress repository. Click the menu item that interests you, and browse the themes.

The final option in the menu is the "Feature Filter". This is where you can filter out the free themes according to features you want to have.

For example, if I wanted to search for a three-column theme that allows a custom header, then I'd search for:

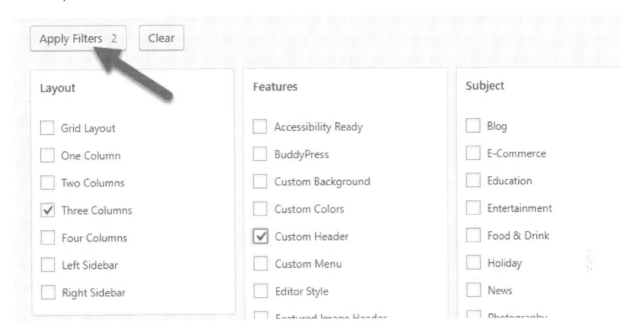

On clicking the **Apply Filters** button, any matches are displayed and appear in the search results:

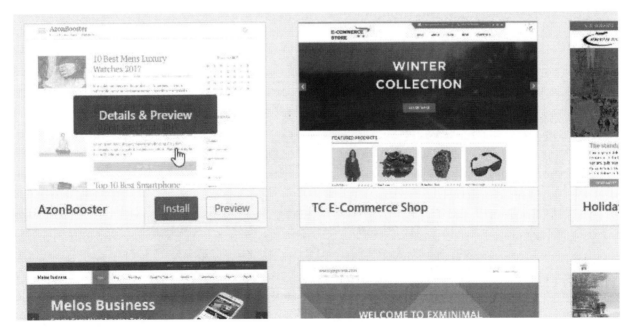

Mouse over each theme in turn to show details for the theme. From this preview, you can:

1. Click **Details & Preview** (or just the Preview button) to get more information about the theme, including a preview.
2. Click the **Install button** to install the theme into your Dashboard.

Note that when you install a new theme, your old one remains in the dashboard. This makes it easy to switch between themes you've installed.

The biggest problem with a lot of free themes is that they have a link back to the creator's website in the footer. This is bad from a search engine point of view, and I do not recommend you use any theme that forces this link on your site.

The WordPress themes we saw earlier do contain links to WordPress, but that is a little different. WordPress is a huge authority site, the creators of the theme and creators of your content management system (CMS). Besides, you can remove that link if you want to.

Customizing a theme

WordPress has a simple point and click interface to help you customize your active theme. However, the customizations that are available to you are dictated by the theme itself. Some themes have very few customizations, while others will offer you pages and pages of custom settings.

There are a couple of ways you can get to the Customize screen. The first is by clicking the **Customize** button on the thumbnail of the active theme in the Themes screen:

The second method is by using the sidebar menu of the Dashboard, where you will find **Customize** in the **Appearance** menu:

Both of these options will open up the "customize" screen:

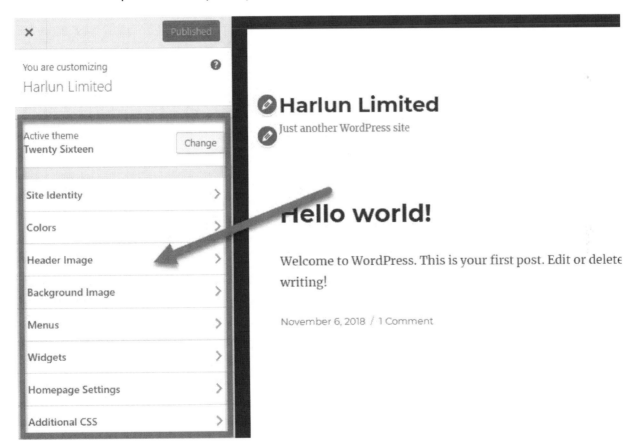

The customization options are on the left of the screen, and a live preview of your site on the right. This allows you to tweak your theme and immediately see the effects of those tweaks in the live preview.

Many of the customizations available here are also accessible via the standard sidebar menus in WordPress (mainly through the **Settings** menu).

Remember that these customization options are specific to the theme you are using. You may see different options for your theme.

The options are grouped into related items. To open these groups, click on the little arrow to the right of the group name. You can explore these options for yourself, but I will mention a couple of items on this customize screen.

Header Image

On this screen, you will be given the dimensions for the header image your theme needs. Make sure your image is sized to those exact dimensions or your header image will look distorted.

The theme above (Twenty Sixteen) requires a header image of 1200 x 280 pixels. If you are looking to add a completely different shaped logo, you may need to find a theme that can accommodate your image. However, you may find a tutorial on Google to show you how to change the size of the expected header image for your chosen theme, so it is worth checking:

Make a Full Width Twenty Sixteen WordPress Theme Header

https://wpbeaches.com/make-a-full-width-twenty-sixteen-header/ ▾

25 Dec 2015 - The CSS background rule also is setting the **image** to not repeat and .... You can also change the **Twenty Sixteen** default **header image size** by ...

Additional CSS

Although CSS is beyond the scope of this book, if you know how to use CSS, you can add custom CSS to style your web pages in this section of the customize options:

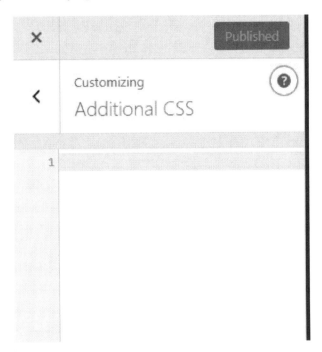

The CSS you add to this box will override the CSS that is built into your theme.

Go through the rest of the options on the customize screen. You won't break anything in this area of WordPress, so have fun and explore.

Website Structure

Remember earlier in the book when we discussed when to use posts and when to use pages? I want to revisit that discussion here as you now have a better understanding of how WordPress works.

If I was building out the WordPress tutorials website used as an example in this book, I would choose a site structure similar to that shown below:

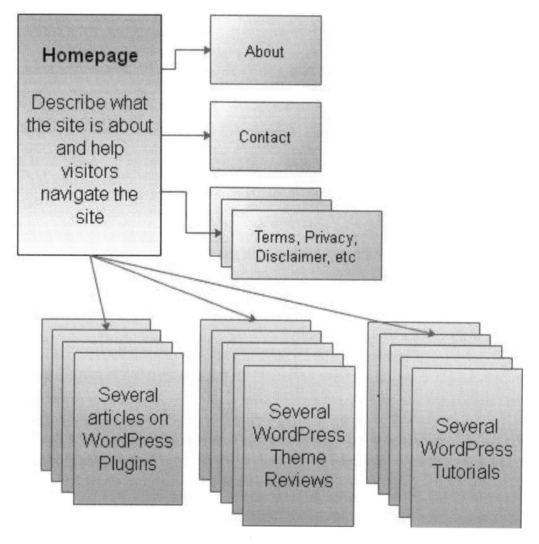

We have a homepage and several "legal" pages created using WordPress pages. We then have a few categories, each containing relevant posts (created using WordPress posts).

The other type of site we mentioned earlier uses WordPress pages as the main content, not posts. WordPress posts are then typically reserved for the site's blog. Here is that structure:

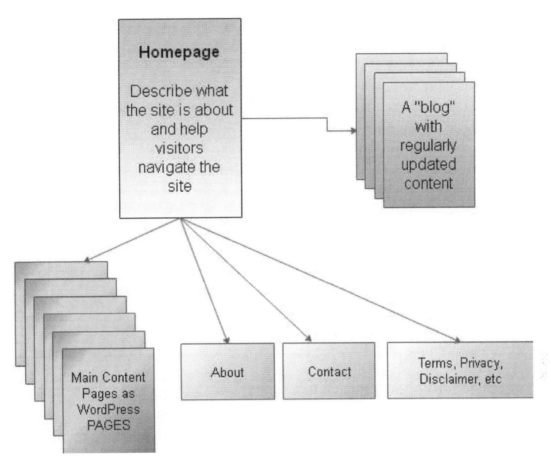

This type of site is typically a small site, with 5 or 6 main content "static" pages plus legal pages. The blog is then used for regular updates on any topic relevant to the blog.

Let's look at an example.

If you were an author, a small website could help showcase your books and offer a little more information about you and your interests to your readers. A contact form would allow your readers to have direct contact with you, and comments on posts would allow a two-way dialogue (a unique opportunity for many authors, since most never get to meet the people that buy their books).

You might want to have the following pages on your site:

- About
- Contact
- My Books
- Events

These could all be set up as WordPress Pages because they are all fairly independent of one another.

You might then want to have a blog where you can post short stories, interesting anecdotes, interesting background information on stories you are writing, etc. If these were done with posts, your visitors could then leave comments and interact with you and give you feedback on your work.

In this scenario, it makes perfect sense to use WordPress pages for the small number of static pages on your site, and WordPress posts for more regular updates and interacting with your readers.

We already know how to set up pages, so setting up the basic structure of this site is easy. Just create a WordPress page for each of those 4 pages we mentioned above.

For the blog, you might just like to use one category or several. This will depend on what you intend to do with the blog. Whatever you choose, WordPress makes it easy to showcase your blog postings.

The first step is to create a new WordPress Page called "Blog" (or whatever you want to call it). Leave the contents of the page empty and publish it.

Now, under the **Settings** menu, click **Reading**.

In the same way, we set the homepage to be a static page, we can set a static page to showcase our "posts", which in this case is the author's "blog" section.

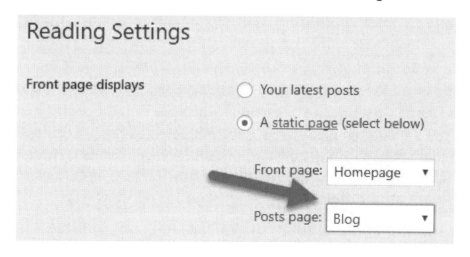

Just select your Blog page from the **Posts page** section of the form, and save changes.

The author could now create the website top navigation menu to include a link to the blog page. Visitors clicking on that would see all of the latest blog posts (from all categories if there is more than one) in chronological order, starting with the most recent.

This is the menu bar from the site of an author I know:

He has used WordPress pages for his About, Books, Interests, Links, Contact &
Disclaimer. He then created a WordPress Page to host his blog posts and added all of
these pages to the top navigation menu.

Even though one page is dedicated to all blog posts, if you use multiple categories for
your posts, you can still use a category widget (if you want to) to help your visitors
find specific posts.

NOTE: Anyone can set up a "Blog" page if they want a single location to display all
recent posts in chronological order. On a traditional WordPress site where the latest
10 posts are shown on the homepage, this type of blog page is not really needed
because your homepage acts as a blog page. However, if you use a static page for
your homepage, then a blog page might be useful for your visitors.

The Structure is Limited Only by Your Imagination

I use posts for the main content on all websites I own. However, I often want to have
a blog as well as the main content. Something like this:

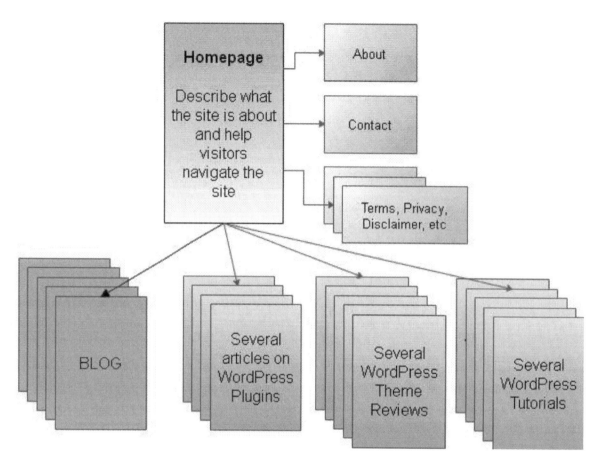

It's the structure you saw earlier, but it has a separate blog where I can post short, relevant, time-sensitive information. In this case, the blog page is no good for me, as it would also contain all of the main content that I created as posts. Can you think of a solution?

It's actually very easy. Create a post category called "blog", and then just file your blog posts into that category. Since WordPress creates a category page for each category you create, you'll now have a blog category page which you can link to as "Blog" in a menu.

Beginner's Mistakes

There are a number of simple mistakes that beginners make when they build a site with WordPress. This chapter lists some of those mistakes.

Post & Page Titles

No two posts should have the same title on your site. No two pages should have the same title either. A post should not use the same title as a page, and vice versa. All post and pages must have unique titles.

If you use the same title on two documents, Google will think you have two articles on the same topic and wonder why. When Google starts getting confused about the content on your site, you are at the beginning of a very slippery slope.

In addition, if you give two posts the same title, the filename automatically generated by WordPress will mean both filenames are nearly the same. WordPress handles duplicate filenames by adding numbers to the end. If you created three pages with the title "contact", WordPress would give them these filenames:

1. Contact
2. Contact-1
3. Contact-2

Tags & Category Names

Never use the same word or phrase for a category name AND a tag. A phrase can be EITHER a category OR a tag, but not both.

Similarly, never use a word or phrase that you have used as a page/post title as either a tag or category.

For example, suppose you had a health site.

If you had a category called diabetes, you could not use the word diabetes as a post/page title, or a tag. You could have a page/post title or tag that included the word diabetes as a longer phrase, like "gestational diabetes", or "pre-diabetes".

Using Tags

Never use more than 4 or 5 tags on a post. Tags should be there to help visitors, so giving visitors long lists of tags will make them useless. Also, indiscriminate use of tags means you'll end up with a lot of tag pages, each listing very few posts. Remember what I said earlier in the book. No tag should be used if it is only being used on one post (or two, and maybe even three depending on the size of your site).

Search Engine Visibility

There is a setting in WordPress that will basically make your site invisible to the search engines.

Go to **Reading** in the **Settings** menu.

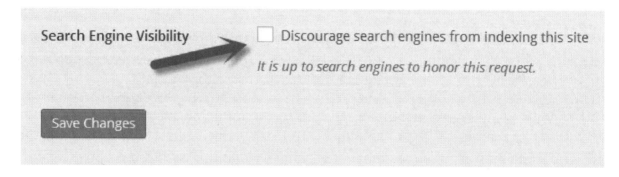

This checkbox is there to stop search engines finding, spidering, and including your site in the search results. Some webmasters use this when they are initially building a site, and then uncheck it when they want to open the site to the public. However, this is not necessary. I'd recommend you leave this unchecked at all times.

If you do find that your site isn't getting indexed and included in Google, do check this setting.

Spam Comments

Over the years, I have seen a number of my students committing this sin. They'll approve a comment on their site, simply because the comment is flattering to them. We've talked about this type of comment before. My advice to you is simple. No matter how few comments you may have, NEVER approve a comment that does not add to the conversation of the post it will appear on.

NEVER!

No really. I mean it.

NEVER!

Plugins for all occasions

We have already installed and used some great WordPress plugins. However, there are thousands more out there. In this chapter, I'll list the plugins that I have found to be the most useful on my own sites. Some of these plugins are used on all of my WordPress sites, while others are only used for more specific projects.

To keep this book shorter, I will list the most important plugins I use regularly, with a description of what they do.

Yoast SEO

Yoast SEO is a free plugin that can help you set up your site with the search engines in mind. SEO stands for Search Engine Optimization, and although we have to be careful implementing SEO strategies on our sites, this plugin is well worth installing. It is an extremely feature-rich plugin that gives you a fine level of control over all posts, pages, tag pages, category pages, etc. I use this on every site I build.

Find it in the plugin repository.

Pretty Link Lite

Pretty Link Lite is a free plugin that allows you to create "prettier" links from longer, "uglier" links. It also allows you to track links.

Why might you want to do this?

We'll mention affiliate programs in the next chapter, and these have notoriously ugly long links. Pretty Link Lite is a great way to make those links more manageable.

Find it in the plugin repository.

CI Backlinks

CI Backlinks is a commercial plugin that I helped develop, which automates internal site linking in the body of your articles. Internal site links help your visitors find their way around your site (check out this type of linking on Wikipedia) but also help the search engines spider your site, and decide what the web pages on your site are about.

http://ezseonews.com/cibacklinks

Dynamic Widgets

Dynamic widgets is a free plugin that allows you to choose specific pages, posts, categories etc. to display widgets on. I use this on most of my sites so that I can create custom sidebars for different categories on the site. If someone is reading a post on my site about web hosting, I can make sure that they see web hosting related advertising in the sidebar.

I also usually create a unique sidebar for my homepage.

I believe that Google prefers websites that don't have the exact same sidebars & footers on all web pages. This plugin helps you achieve that since you can control which widgets appear on which pages, and in which widgetized areas of the page.

Find it in the plugin repository.

W3 Total Cache

W3 Total Cache is a free plugin to speed up your site. It is a little complicated to set up but well worth the effort.

Find it in the plugin repository.

Wishlist Member

Wishlist Member is a commercial plugin that allows you to set up a membership site (paid or free) on your website. I use it for the training programs and courses that I create.

https://ezseonews.com/wlm

wpForo Forum

wpForo Forum is a free plugin that allows you to set up a forum on your site. If you want to grow a community on your website, this plugin can create a forum on your site, with a few mouse clicks.

Making Money with your website

There are a lot of different ways you can make money with your website. I won't go into too much detail in this book, but I will briefly discuss the options.

All of the following forms of site monetization are free to join and do not cost anything to run on your website.

Affiliate programs

An affiliate program (sometimes called a partner program) is a good way to make some money from your site. A lot of great companies run them, and you can apply to join relevant programs.

Amazon has a great affiliate program. When you join, you can link to any product on the Amazon website from your own website, using a link that Amazon gives you. This link is long and ugly, which is where Pretty Link Lite comes in. If someone goes through your link and buys something, you get a commission.

The amount of commission you get with affiliate programs varies enormously. For example, Amazon pays around 4% - 8% of the order value, but they convert customers very well.

Other sites like Clickbank specialize in digital products (eBooks & software). The average commission is probably around 50%, but you can earn 75% commission on some products, sometimes even more than that.

Shareasale and Commission Junction are two affiliate networks I use. An affiliate network is a company that works with other companies that want to run an affiliate program. You can sign up at Shareasale and/or Commission Junction (often just referred to as CJ), then apply to join affiliate programs on their books. Some affiliate programs will accept you immediately; others require a manual review of your site and application. However, it is typically very easy to join affiliate programs through both of these networks. If you make a commission on a network, the network collects the commissions for you and then pays you every month.

Google Adsense

When you visit Google and search for something, the top few results are typically adverts related to what you searched for. Companies are paying for these adverts.

If you click on one of these adverts in Google, the company that paid for the advert pays Google some money. The amount they have to pay is based on the "cost per click" (or CPC) value of that advert. Adverts in more competitive niches cost more, so the CPC is higher.

Google Adsense is a program that allows you to put similar "Adsense" adverts on your website. When someone clicks on one of these Adsense adverts on your site, Google gets paid the CPC by the company that owns the advert. Google then share this money with you.

Where to Go from Here?

We've covered a lot of ground in this book. You should now be confident finding your way around the WordPress Dashboard. However, many of you will want to go on and expand your knowledge of WordPress. I've therefore listed some useful resources below.

My Other Webmaster Books

All my books are available as Kindle books and paperbacks. You can view them all here:

http://amazon.com/author/drandrewwilliams

I'll leave you to explore those if you are interested. You'll find books on various aspects of being a webmaster, such as creating high-quality content, SEO, CSS etc.

My Video Courses

I have a growing number of video courses hosted on Udemy. You can view a complete list of these at my site:

https://ezseonews.com/udemy

There are courses on the same kinds of topics that my books cover, so SEO, Content Creation, WordPress, Website Analytics, etc.

Google Webmaster Guidelines

https://ezseonews.com/wmg – this is the webmaster's bible of what is acceptable and what is not in the eyes of the world's biggest search engine.

Google Analytics

http://www.google.com/analytics/ – the best free analytics program out there. When you have some free time to learn how to use Google Analytics, I recommend you add it to your site so you can track your visitors.

Did you enjoy this book?

If you liked this book (or even if you didn't), PLEASE add a review on the Amazon website. It provides me with valuable feedback and helps prospective students decide whether it is the right book for them.

All the best

Andy Williams

74554305R00107

Made in the USA
Columbia, SC
12 September 2019